Enterprise Arc Fundamentals

A book by

Ian Loe

First edition 2024

Dedication

To those who envision the future with clarity and build it with dedication:

This book is dedicated to the architects of change, the pioneers of innovation, and the custodians of knowledge. Your unwavering commitment to shaping robust, resilient, and adaptable architectures inspires us all. May this work serve as a beacon of insight and a tool for excellence in the ever-evolving landscape of enterprise architecture.

To the mentors who guided my path, the colleagues who shared their wisdom, and the readers who seek to advance their craft—this is for you.

Table of Contents

INTRODUCTION 1

WHAT DO ARCHITECTS DO? 2
ARCHITECTS AS OBSERVERS OF BEHAVIOUR 3
CREATING SPACE FOR PATTERNS OF BEHAVIOUR TO FLOURISH 4
EMERGENCE OF A LANGUAGE OF PATTERNS 5
EXPANDING THE VOCABULARY OF PATTERN LANGUAGE IN IT ARCHITECTURE 5
THE IMPORTANCE OF ENTERPRISE ARCHITECTURE 6
THE EVOLUTION OF ENTERPRISE ARCHITECTURE 7
THE STRATEGIC ROLE OF ENTERPRISE ARCHITECTURE 8
THE VALUE OF ENTERPRISE ARCHITECTURE IN DECISION-MAKING 9
THE FUTURE OF ENTERPRISE ARCHITECTURE 10

EVOLUTION OF ENTERPRISE ARCHITECTURE 11

THE ORIGINS OF ENTERPRISE ARCHITECTURE 12
THE EVOLUTION OF ENTERPRISE ARCHITECTURE IN THE 1990S 13
THE RISE OF GOVERNMENT AND INDUSTRY-SPECIFIC FRAMEWORKS 14
THE EXPANSION OF ENTERPRISE ARCHITECTURE IN THE 2000S 16
THE IMPACT OF DIGITAL TRANSFORMATION 17
THE FUTURE OF ENTERPRISE ARCHITECTURE 18

SOME ENTERPRISE ARCHITECTURE FRAMEWORKS 20

THE ZACHMAN FRAMEWORK 21
THE OPEN GROUP ARCHITECTURE FRAMEWORK (TOGAF) 21
FEDERAL ENTERPRISE ARCHITECTURE FRAMEWORK (FEAF) 21
GARTNER'S ENTERPRISE ARCHITECTURE FRAMEWORK 22
THE MINISTRY OF DEFENCE ARCHITECTURE FRAMEWORK (MODAF) 22

THE DRAGON1 FRAMEWORK 22

THE ZACHMAN FRAMEWORK 23

HISTORY OF THE ZACHMAN FRAMEWORK 23
STRUCTURE OF THE ZACHMAN FRAMEWORK 25
THE COLUMN - ARCHITECTURAL ASPECTS 25
THE ROWS - STAKEHOLDER PERSPECTIVES 26
HOW THE ZACHMAN FRAMEWORK IS USED 28
EXAMPLES OF USING THE ZACHMAN FRAMEWORK 29
EXAMPLE 1: DATA MANAGEMENT 29
EXAMPLE 2: PROCESS AUTOMATION 34
STRENGTHS OF THE ZACHMAN FRAMEWORK 39
COMPREHENSIVE COVERAGE ACROSS MULTIPLE DIMENSIONS 39
VERSATILITY ACROSS INDUSTRIES AND ORGANISATIONS 40
IMPROVED COMMUNICATION AND COLLABORATION 40
ALIGNMENT OF BUSINESS AND IT 41
MANAGEMENT OF COMPLEXITY 41
LIMITATIONS OF THE ZACHMAN FRAMEWORK 42
COMPLEXITY AND DIFFICULTY IN IMPLEMENTATION 42
LACK OF PRESCRIPTIVE GUIDANCE 42
STATIC NATURE AND DIFFICULTY IN ADAPTATION 43
TOOL-AGNOSTIC NATURE 43
POTENTIAL FOR OVER-DOCUMENTATION 44
MISALIGNMENT WITH AGILE AND LEAN PRACTICES 44

THE OPEN GROUP ARCHITECTURE FRAMEWORK (TOGAF) 46

HISTORY OF TOGAF 46
HOW TOGAF IS USED FOR ENTERPRISE ARCHITECTURE 47

THE ARCHITECTURE DEVELOPMENT METHOD (ADM) 48

TOGAF'S ARCHITECTURE CONTENT FRAMEWORK 50

TOGAF'S ENTERPRISE CONTINUUM 51

GOVERNANCE AND COMPLIANCE 52

EXAMPLES OF TOGAF IN USE **53**

EXAMPLE 1: FINANCIAL INSTITUTION MODERNISATION 53

EXAMPLE 2: GOVERNMENT AGENCY TRANSFORMATION 54

STRENGTHS OF TOGAF **55**

COMPREHENSIVE AND STRUCTURED APPROACH 55

FLEXIBILITY AND ADAPTABILITY 55

FOCUS ON GOVERNANCE AND COMPLIANCE 55

ENCOURAGES REUSE OF ARCHITECTURAL ASSETS 56

WIDELY RECOGNISED AND SUPPORTED 56

LIMITATIONS OF TOGAF **56**

COMPLEXITY AND STEEP LEARNING CURVE 56

POTENTIAL FOR OVER-DOCUMENTATION 57

LACK OF PRESCRIPTIVE TOOLS AND TECHNIQUES 57

NOT EASILY ALIGNED WITH AGILE PRACTICES 58

FOCUS ON LARGE ENTERPRISES 58

FEDERAL ENTERPRISE ARCHITECTURE FRAMEWORK (FEAF) **60**

HISTORY OF FEAF **61**

HOW FEAF IS USED FOR ENTERPRISE ARCHITECTURE **63**

ESTABLISHING A GOVERNANCE STRUCTURE 63

DEFINING THE SCOPE AND OBJECTIVES 64

ENGAGING STAKEHOLDERS 64

DEVELOPING THE ARCHITECTURE 65

IMPLEMENTING THE ARCHITECTURE 65

CONTINUOUS IMPROVEMENT AND EVOLUTION 66

ENSURING COMPLIANCE AND REPORTING 66

LEVERAGING BEST PRACTICES AND LESSONS LEARNED 67

EXAMPLES OF FEAF IN USE **67**

EXAMPLE 1: DEPARTMENT OF HOMELAND SECURITY (DHS) 67

EXAMPLE 2: ENVIRONMENTAL PROTECTION AGENCY (EPA) 68

EXAMPLE 3: DEPARTMENT OF DEFENCE (DoD) 68

STRENGTHS OF FEAF **68**

STANDARDISATION AND INTEROPERABILITY 69

ALIGNMENT WITH STRATEGIC GOALS 69

FOCUS ON EFFICIENCY AND COST-EFFECTIVENESS 69

COMPREHENSIVE GOVERNANCE AND COMPLIANCE FRAMEWORK 70

SCALABILITY AND FLEXIBILITY 70

LIMITATIONS OF FEAF **70**

COMPLEXITY AND RESOURCE REQUIREMENTS 71

POTENTIAL FOR OVER-DOCUMENTATION 71

DIFFICULTY IN ADAPTING TO AGILE AND MODERN PRACTICES 71

LIMITED FOCUS ON EMERGING TECHNOLOGIES 72

RISK OF SILOED IMPLEMENTATION 72

GARTNER'S ENTERPRISE ARCHITECTURE FRAMEWORK **74**

HISTORY OF GARTNER'S ENTERPRISE ARCHITECTURE FRAMEWORK **74**

HOW GARTNER'S ENTERPRISE ARCHITECTURE FRAMEWORK IS USED **76**

STRATEGIC ALIGNMENT OF BUSINESS AND IT 76

ENABLING DIGITAL TRANSFORMATION 76

MANAGING COMPLEXITY IN IT ENVIRONMENTS 77

GOVERNANCE AND DECISION-MAKING 77

EXAMPLES OF GARTNER'S FRAMEWORK IN USE **78**

EXAMPLE 1: A GLOBAL FINANCIAL INSTITUTION 79

EXAMPLE 2: LARGE MANUFACTURING COMPANY 81

STRENGTHS OF GARTNER'S ENTERPRISE ARCHITECTURE FRAMEWORK   **83**

BUSINESS OUTCOME-FOCUSED   83

FLEXIBILITY AND ADAPTABILITY   84

SUPPORT FOR DIGITAL TRANSFORMATION   84

COMPREHENSIVE AND HOLISTIC VIEW   84

EMPHASIS ON AGILITY   85

LIMITATIONS OF GARTNER'S ENTERPRISE ARCHITECTURE FRAMEWORK   **85**

REQUIRES STRONG LEADERSHIP AND SUPPORT   85

RESOURCE-INTENSIVE   85

COMPLEXITY IN LARGE ORGANISATIONS   86

POTENTIAL FOR OVER-ANALYSIS   86

INTEGRATION WITH AGILE METHODOLOGIES   86

MINISTRY OF DEFENCE ARCHITECTURE FRAMEWORK (MODAF)

88

HISTORY OF MODAF   **89**

HOW MODAF IS USED BY ORGANISATIONS   **90**

DESIGN AND DEVELOPMENT OF DEFENCE SYSTEMS   91

STRATEGIC PLANNING AND DECISION-MAKING   91

COMMUNICATION AND COLLABORATION   92

LIFECYCLE MANAGEMENT OF DEFENCE SYSTEMS   93

STRENGTHS OF MODAF   **93**

TAILORED FOR DEFENCE NEEDS   93

COMPREHENSIVE AND STRUCTURED APPROACH   94

ENSURES INTEROPERABILITY   94

FACILITATES STRATEGIC PLANNING   94

SUPPORTS LIFECYCLE MANAGEMENT   95

LIMITATIONS OF MODAF   **95**

COMPLEXITY   95

RESOURCE INTENSIVE 96

FOCUS ON DEFENCE SECTOR 96

RIGID STRUCTURE 96

EVOLVING NEEDS AND TECHNOLOGY 97

DRAGON1 FRAMEWORK 98

HISTORY OF THE DRAGON1 FRAMEWORK 99

HOW DRAGON1 IS USED 100

VISUALISING ENTERPRISE ARCHITECTURE 101

ALIGNING BUSINESS AND IT 101

MANAGING COMPLEXITY 102

EXAMPLES OF DRAGON1 103

EXAMPLE 1: FINANCIAL SERVICES COMPANY 103

EXAMPLE 2: HEALTHCARE ORGANISATION 104

STRENGTHS OF THE DRAGON1 FRAMEWORK 105

EMPHASIS ON VISUALISATION 105

BUSINESS-DRIVEN APPROACH 105

FLEXIBILITY AND ADAPTABILITY 105

SUPPORT FOR TRANSFORMATION AND INNOVATION 106

LIMITATIONS OF THE DRAGON1 FRAMEWORK 106

LEARNING CURVE 106

RESOURCE REQUIREMENTS 107

FOCUS ON VISUALISATION 107

ORGANISING AN ENTERPRISE ARCHITECTURE TEAM 108

IT ARCHITECTURE: A CONCEPTUAL OVERVIEW 109

CHIEF ARCHITECT 112

SETTING THE STRATEGIC DIRECTION FOR ENTERPRISE ARCHITECTURE 112

Aligning Technology with Business Goals 112

Identifying Future Trends and Opportunities 113

Developing a Multi-Year Architectural Roadmap 113

OVERSEEING THE DEVELOPMENT AND IMPLEMENTATION OF ARCHITECTURE

113

Architectural Governance and Standards 114

Managing Cross-Functional Teams 114

Ensuring Flexibility and Scalability 114

Risk Management and Mitigation 115

COMMUNICATING THE ARCHITECTURE TO SENIOR LEADERSHIP AND

STAKEHOLDERS 115

Articulating the Value of Architecture 115

Facilitating Stakeholder Engagement 115

Providing Regular Updates and Reports 116

Driving Architectural Decisions and Approvals 116

ENTERPRISE ARCHITECT **118**

BUSINESS ARCHITECT **119**

TECHNOLOGY ARCHITECT **120**

INFORMATION ARCHITECT **121**

SECURITY ARCHITECT **122**

INTEGRATION ARCHITECT **123**

SOLUTIONS ARCHITECT **125**

APPLICATION ARCHITECT **126**

ARCHITECTURE COMPETENCIES **128**

THE ENTERPRISE ARCHITECT **130**

SKILLS NECESSARY FOR AN ENTERPRISE ARCHITECT **131**

TECHNICAL PROFICIENCY 132

BUSINESS ACUMEN 133

COMMUNICATION AND LEADERSHIP 134
ANALYTICAL AND PROBLEM-SOLVING SKILLS 135
ADAPTABILITY AND CONTINUOUS LEARNING 135
HOW AN ENTERPRISE ARCHITECT PERFORMS THEIR JOB **136**
ASSESSING THE CURRENT STATE 137
DEVELOPING THE TARGET ARCHITECTURE 138
CREATING A ROADMAP AND IMPLEMENTATION PLAN 138
LEADING AND SUPPORTING IMPLEMENTATION 139
ENSURING GOVERNANCE AND COMPLIANCE 140
COMMUNICATING AND ADVOCATING 140
BEST PRACTICES FOR SUCCESS AS AN ENTERPRISE ARCHITECT **141**
ALIGN ARCHITECTURE WITH BUSINESS STRATEGY 142
ENGAGE STAKEHOLDERS EARLY AND OFTEN 142
EMBRACE CONTINUOUS LEARNING 142
PRIORITISE AGILITY AND FLEXIBILITY 143
LEVERAGE DATA AND ANALYTICS 143
FOCUS ON COMMUNICATION AND COLLABORATION 144
MAINTAIN A LONG-TERM PERSPECTIVE 144
IMPLEMENT ROBUST GOVERNANCE 144
LEARNING EXERCISES TO DEVELOP ENTERPRISE ARCHITECTURE SKILLS **145**
CASE STUDY ANALYSIS 145
SIMULATION EXERCISES 146
FRAMEWORK MASTERY 146
CROSS-FUNCTIONAL COLLABORATION 147

THE BUSINESS ARCHITECT **148**

SKILLS NECESSARY FOR A BUSINESS ARCHITECT **149**
STRATEGIC THINKING 150
ANALYTICAL AND PROBLEM-SOLVING SKILLS 151

COMMUNICATION AND COLLABORATION 151

CHANGE MANAGEMENT 152

TECHNICAL KNOWLEDGE 153

HOW A BUSINESS ARCHITECT PERFORMS THEIR JOB **153**

UNDERSTANDING THE BUSINESS STRATEGY 154

ANALYSING AND MODELLING BUSINESS PROCESSES: 154

DEVELOPING BUSINESS ARCHITECTURE 154

ENGAGING STAKEHOLDERS 155

LEADING CHANGE MANAGEMENT 155

MONITORING AND CONTINUOUS IMPROVEMENT 155

BEST PRACTICES FOR SUCCESS AS A BUSINESS ARCHITECT **156**

ALIGN BUSINESS ARCHITECTURE WITH STRATEGIC GOALS 156

ENGAGE STAKEHOLDERS EARLY AND OFTEN 157

PRIORITISE COMMUNICATION AND COLLABORATION 157

EMBRACE CONTINUOUS LEARNING 158

FOCUS ON DATA-DRIVEN DECISION MAKING 158

BE AGILE AND FLEXIBLE 159

IMPLEMENT ROBUST CHANGE MANAGEMENT 159

LEARNING EXERCISES TO DEVELOP BUSINESS ARCHITECTURE SKILLS **159**

CASE STUDY ANALYSIS 160

PROCESS MODELLING WORKSHOPS 160

CROSS-FUNCTIONAL PROJECTS 160

FRAMEWORK MASTERY 160

CHANGE MANAGEMENT SIMULATIONS 161

THE TECHNOLOGY ARCHITECT **162**

SKILLS NECESSARY FOR A TECHNOLOGY ARCHITECT **163**

TECHNICAL PROFICIENCY 164

STRATEGIC PLANNING AND DESIGN 165

PROBLEM-SOLVING AND INNOVATION 166
COMMUNICATION AND LEADERSHIP 166
HOW A TECHNOLOGY ARCHITECT PERFORMS THEIR JOB **167**
ASSESSING THE CURRENT INFRASTRUCTURE 168
DESIGNING THE TARGET ARCHITECTURE 169
CREATING A ROADMAP AND IMPLEMENTATION PLAN 169
LEADING IMPLEMENTATION AND TROUBLESHOOTING 169
ENSURING SECURITY AND COMPLIANCE 170
CONTINUOUS MONITORING AND OPTIMISATION 170
BEST PRACTICES FOR SUCCESS AS A TECHNOLOGY ARCHITECT **171**
ALIGN TECHNOLOGY ARCHITECTURE WITH BUSINESS GOALS 171
PRIORITISE SECURITY AND COMPLIANCE 172
EMBRACE CONTINUOUS LEARNING AND INNOVATION 172
FOCUS ON COMMUNICATION AND COLLABORATION 172
BE PROACTIVE IN PROBLEM-SOLVING 172
DESIGN FOR SCALABILITY AND FLEXIBILITY 173
LEARNING EXERCISES TO DEVELOP TECHNOLOGY ARCHITECTURE SKILLS

173
CASE STUDY ANALYSIS 173
TECHNOLOGY SIMULATION EXERCISES 173
SECURITY AND COMPLIANCE WORKSHOPS 174
EMERGING TECHNOLOGY RESEARCH 174
CROSS-FUNCTIONAL COLLABORATION PROJECTS 174

THE INFORMATION ARCHITECT **175**

SKILLS NECESSARY FOR AN INFORMATION ARCHITECT **176**
DATA MANAGEMENT AND MODELLING 177
TECHNICAL PROFICIENCY 178
ANALYTICAL AND PROBLEM-SOLVING SKILLS 179

COMMUNICATION AND COLLABORATION 179

HOW AN INFORMATION ARCHITECT PERFORMS THEIR JOB **180**

ASSESSING THE CURRENT DATA LANDSCAPE 181

DESIGNING THE DATA ARCHITECTURE 182

IMPLEMENTING DATA GOVERNANCE 182

COLLABORATING WITH STAKEHOLDERS 182

MONITORING AND OPTIMISING DATA ARCHITECTURE 183

BEST PRACTICES FOR SUCCESS AS AN INFORMATION ARCHITECT **184**

ALIGN DATA ARCHITECTURE WITH BUSINESS STRATEGY 184

PRIORITISE DATA GOVERNANCE 184

EMBRACE CONTINUOUS LEARNING AND INNOVATION 185

FOCUS ON COMMUNICATION AND COLLABORATION 185

DESIGN FOR SCALABILITY AND FLEXIBILITY 185

LEARNING EXERCISES TO DEVELOP INFORMATION ARCHITECTURE SKILLS

186

DATA MODELLING WORKSHOPS 186

DATA GOVERNANCE SIMULATIONS 186

CASE STUDY ANALYSIS 186

DATABASE TECHNOLOGY RESEARCH 187

CROSS-FUNCTIONAL COLLABORATION PROJECTS 187

THE SECURITY ARCHITECT **188**

SKILLS NECESSARY FOR A SECURITY ARCHITECT **189**

TECHNICAL PROFICIENCY 190

RISK MANAGEMENT AND COMPLIANCE 191

ANALYTICAL AND PROBLEM-SOLVING SKILLS 192

STRATEGIC PLANNING AND DESIGN 192

COMMUNICATION AND COLLABORATION 193

HOW A SECURITY ARCHITECT PERFORMS THEIR JOB **194**

ASSESSING THE CURRENT SECURITY POSTURE 195

DESIGNING THE SECURITY ARCHITECTURE 195

IMPLEMENTING SECURITY MEASURES 195

CONDUCTING RISK ASSESSMENTS AND COMPLIANCE AUDITS 196

RESPONDING TO SECURITY INCIDENTS 196

CONTINUOUS MONITORING AND IMPROVEMENT 197

BEST PRACTICES FOR SUCCESS AS A SECURITY ARCHITECT **197**

ALIGN SECURITY WITH BUSINESS OBJECTIVES 198

PRIORITISE RISK MANAGEMENT AND COMPLIANCE 198

STAY INFORMED ABOUT EMERGING THREATS 198

FOCUS ON COMMUNICATION AND COLLABORATION 198

DESIGN FOR SCALABILITY AND FLEXIBILITY 199

LEARNING EXERCISES TO DEVELOP SECURITY ARCHITECTURE SKILLS **199**

CYBERSECURITY CERTIFICATION COURSES 199

RISK ASSESSMENT SIMULATIONS 200

COMPLIANCE AUDITS 200

THREAT MODELLING WORKSHOPS 200

CROSS-FUNCTIONAL SECURITY PROJECTS: 200

THE INTEGRATION ARCHITECT **201**

SKILLS NECESSARY FOR AN INTEGRATION ARCHITECT **202**

TECHNICAL PROFICIENCY 203

ANALYTICAL AND PROBLEM-SOLVING SKILLS 204

DESIGN AND ARCHITECTURE 205

COMMUNICATION AND COLLABORATION 205

HOW AN INTEGRATION ARCHITECT PERFORMS THEIR JOB **206**

ASSESSING INTEGRATION NEEDS 207

DESIGNING INTEGRATION SOLUTIONS 208

IMPLEMENTING INTEGRATION PROJECTS 208

MONITORING AND OPTIMISING INTEGRATIONS 208

ENSURING SECURITY AND COMPLIANCE 209

COLLABORATING WITH STAKEHOLDERS 209

BEST PRACTICES FOR SUCCESS AS AN INTEGRATION ARCHITECT **209**

ALIGN INTEGRATION SOLUTIONS WITH BUSINESS OBJECTIVES 210

PRIORITISE SECURITY AND COMPLIANCE: 210

EMBRACE CONTINUOUS LEARNING AND INNOVATION: 210

FOCUS ON COMMUNICATION AND COLLABORATION 211

DESIGN FOR SCALABILITY AND FLEXIBILITY: 211

LEARNING EXERCISES TO DEVELOP INTEGRATION ARCHITECTURE SKILLS

211

INTEGRATION TECHNOLOGY WORKSHOPS 212

CASE STUDY ANALYSIS 212

SECURITY AND COMPLIANCE AUDITS 212

SIMULATION EXERCISES 212

CROSS-FUNCTIONAL COLLABORATION PROJECTS 213

THE SOLUTIONS ARCHITECT **214**

SKILLS NECESSARY FOR A SOLUTIONS ARCHITECT **215**

TECHNICAL PROFICIENCY 216

BUSINESS ACUMEN 217

ANALYTICAL AND PROBLEM-SOLVING SKILLS 218

COMMUNICATION AND COLLABORATION 218

HOW A SOLUTIONS ARCHITECT PERFORMS THEIR JOB **219**

UNDERSTANDING BUSINESS REQUIREMENTS 220

DESIGNING THE SOLUTION 221

DEVELOPING A TECHNICAL ROADMAP 221

OVERSEEING IMPLEMENTATION 221

ENSURING QUALITY AND COMPLIANCE 222

CONTINUOUS IMPROVEMENT 222
BEST PRACTICES FOR SUCCESS AS A SOLUTIONS ARCHITECT 223
ALIGN SOLUTIONS WITH BUSINESS STRATEGY 223
PRIORITISE SCALABILITY AND FLEXIBILITY 223
EMBRACE CONTINUOUS LEARNING AND INNOVATION 224
FOCUS ON COMMUNICATION AND COLLABORATION 224
DOCUMENT AND STANDARDISE SOLUTIONS 224
LEARNING EXERCISES TO DEVELOP SOLUTIONS ARCHITECTURE SKILLS 225
CASE STUDY ANALYSIS 225
ARCHITECTURE DESIGN WORKSHOPS 225
TECHNICAL ROADMAP DEVELOPMENT 225
COLLABORATION AND COMMUNICATION EXERCISES 226
TECHNOLOGY RESEARCH AND PROTOTYPING 226

THE APPLICATION ARCHITECT 227

SKILLS NECESSARY FOR AN APPLICATION ARCHITECT 228
TECHNICAL PROFICIENCY 229
DESIGN AND ARCHITECTURE 230
PROBLEM-SOLVING AND ANALYTICAL SKILLS 231
COMMUNICATION AND COLLABORATION 231
HOW AN APPLICATION ARCHITECT PERFORMS THEIR JOB 232
UNDERSTANDING BUSINESS REQUIREMENTS 233
DESIGNING THE APPLICATION ARCHITECTURE 234
SELECTING TECHNOLOGIES AND TOOLS 234
OVERSEEING DEVELOPMENT AND IMPLEMENTATION 234
ENSURING QUALITY AND COMPLIANCE 235
CONTINUOUS IMPROVEMENT 235
BEST PRACTICES FOR SUCCESS AS AN APPLICATION ARCHITECT 236
ALIGN APPLICATIONS WITH BUSINESS STRATEGY 236

PRIORITISE SCALABILITY AND FLEXIBILITY   237
EMBRACE CONTINUOUS LEARNING AND INNOVATION   237
FOCUS ON COMMUNICATION AND COLLABORATION   237
DOCUMENT AND STANDARDISE APPLICATION ARCHITECTURES   237
LEARNING EXERCISES TO DEVELOP APPLICATION ARCHITECTURE SKILLS

                                                               238
ARCHITECTURE DESIGN WORKSHOPS   238
CODE REVIEW AND REFACTORING EXERCISES   238
TECHNOLOGY RESEARCH AND PROTOTYPING   239
COLLABORATION AND COMMUNICATION EXERCISES   239
CASE STUDY ANALYSIS   239

ARCHITECTURAL THINKING   **240**

ARCHITECT VS. ENGINEER: A DISTINCT PERSPECTIVE   **241**
SOLVING PROBLEMS AT DIFFERENT LEVELS OF COMPLEXITY   **242**
HIGH-LEVEL STRATEGIC COMPLEXITY   242
INTERMEDIATE-LEVEL ARCHITECTURAL COMPLEXITY   243
LOW-LEVEL TECHNICAL COMPLEXITY   244
CROSS-LEVEL PROBLEM-SOLVING: BRIDGING STRATEGIC AND TECHNICAL
DOMAINS   245
ADDRESSING MULTI-DIMENSIONAL PROBLEMS: THE SYSTEMS APPROACH 247
A SYSTEMS APPROACH: FOCUSING ON SYSTEMS AS A WHOLE   **248**
KEY PRINCIPLES OF THE SYSTEMS APPROACH   249
Holistic View   249
Interconnected Components   249
Emergent Properties   249
Feedback Loops   250
Alignment with Purpose   250
EXAMPLES OF THE SYSTEMS APPROACH IN PRACTICE   250

Smart City Infrastructure Development 250

Hybrid Cloud Strategy Implementation 251

Enterprise Resource Planning (ERP) System Integration 252

Customer 360 Strategy in a Financial Institution 253

Healthcare Ecosystem Integration 254

PURPOSE: THE CORE OF ARCHITECTURAL THINKING **256**

KEY ASPECTS OF PURPOSE IN ARCHITECTURAL THINKING 257

Alignment with Business Strategy 257

Guiding Design and Integration Choices 257

Driving Innovation and Adaptability 257

Ensuring Consistency Across Systems 258

Facilitating Stakeholder Communication and Buy-In 258

Providing a Framework for Measuring Success 259

EXAMPLES OF PURPOSE-DRIVEN ARCHITECTURE 259

E-Commerce Platform for Rapid Growth 259

Public Sector Data Sharing Initiative 260

Banking Platform for Financial Inclusion 261

HOW MODELLING HELPS IN ARCHITECTURAL THINKING **262**

KEY BENEFITS OF MODELLING IN ARCHITECTURE 262

Clarification of Complex Systems 262

Facilitating Communication and Collaboration 263

Enabling Better Decision-Making and Scenario Analysis: 264

Improving Risk Management and Mitigation 264

Supporting Documentation and Standardisation 265

Driving Alignment with Business Goals 266

Facilitating Agile and Iterative Development: 266

TYPES OF MODELS USED IN ARCHITECTURAL THINKING 268

CONCEPTUAL MODELS 268

LOGICAL MODELS 269

PHYSICAL MODELS 270

PROCESS MODELS 271

DATA MODELS 272

INSIGHTS VS. HEURISTICS: A KEY DISTINCTION IN ARCHITECTURAL
THINKING 273

WHAT ARE INSIGHTS? 274

WHAT ARE HEURISTICS? 275

KEY DIFFERENCES BETWEEN INSIGHTS AND HEURISTICS 276

Nature and Origin 276

Purpose and Application 276

Certainty and Reliability 276

Flexibility and Adaptability: 277

WHEN TO USE INSIGHTS VS. HEURISTICS IN ARCHITECTURE 277

EXAMPLES OF INSIGHTS VS. HEURISTICS IN ARCHITECTURAL PRACTICE 278

Example in Cloud Migration 278

Example in Security Architecture 278

Example in Microservices Design 279

COMBINING INSIGHTS AND HEURISTICS FOR EFFECTIVE ARCHITECTURAL
THINKING 279

ART COMPLEMENTS SCIENCE IN ARCHITECTURE 282

THE ROLE OF ART IN ARCHITECTING 283

CONCEPTUALISATION AND INNOVATION 283

APPLYING PAST EXPERIENCE AND WISDOM 284

SANITY CHECKS AND BALANCING AMBIGUITY 284

HOW THE NATURE OF ARCHITECTING CHANGES ACROSS PHASES 285

EARLIEST STAGES: STRUCTURING HOPES, NEEDS, AND DREAMS 285

Vision and Imagination 285

Synthesising Diverse Inputs 285

Navigating Uncertainty 286

LATER STAGES: INTEGRATION AND MEDIATION AMONG COMPETING
SUBSYSTEMS   286
Normative and Rational Methods   286
Mediating Conflicting Interests   287
Adapting to Changing Requirements   287
THE SYNERGY BETWEEN ART AND SCIENCE IN ARCHITECTURE   **287**
BALANCING TECHNICAL EXCELLENCE WITH HUMAN-CENTRED DESIGN   288
Finding the Right Balance   289
FOSTERING INNOVATION WHILE ENSURING RELIABILITY   290
Knowing When to Innovate and When to Standardise   290
CREATING ENDURING AND ADAPTIVE ARCHITECTURES   291
Art and Science in Future-Proofing   291
Building in Adaptability   292

ARCHITECTURE STANDARD LANGUAGE   **294**

IMPORTANCE OF USING STANDARD LANGUAGE IN ARCHITECTURE   **295**
CLARITY AND PRECISION IN COMMUNICATION   296
CONSISTENCY IN METHODS AND DELIVERABLES   297
FACILITATES COLLABORATION AND REUSE   299
SUPPORTS GOVERNANCE AND COMPLIANCE   301
EVOLUTION OF ARCHITECTURAL LANGUAGE   **302**
EARLY STAGES: FROM FLOWCHARTS TO STRUCTURED DESIGN METHODS   302
THE OBJECT-ORIENTED REVOLUTION: INTRODUCTION OF UML   303
EXPANDING THE SCOPE: THE EMERGENCE OF ENTERPRISE ARCHITECTURE
LANGUAGES   304
MODERN DEVELOPMENTS: INTEGRATION, FLEXIBILITY, AND DIGITAL
TRANSFORMATION   304
FUTURE DIRECTIONS: TOWARDS INTEROPERABILITY AND AUTOMATION   306
Interoperability   306

Automation   306
Collaboration   306
COMMON ARCHITECTURAL LANGUAGES   **307**
UNIFIED MODELLING LANGUAGE (UML)   307
Key Features of UML   307
Evolution of UML   308
ARCHIMATE   308
Evolution of ArchiMate   309
CHOOSING THE RIGHT LANGUAGE FOR YOUR ARCHITECTURE   **309**
FACTORS TO CONSIDER WHEN CHOOSING AN ARCHITECTURAL LANGUAGE

                                                               310
Scope and Focus of the Architecture   310
Audience and Stakeholders   312
Complexity and Level of Detail   313
Tooling and Integration with Existing Practices   314
Need for Integration and Interoperability   315
COMBINING UML AND ARCHIMATE FOR COMPREHENSIVE COVERAGE   316

**ARCHITECTURE BUILDING BLOCKS IN ENTERPRISE
ARCHITECTURE**   **318**

UNDERSTANDING ARCHITECTURE BUILDING BLOCKS (ABBS)   **319**
BUSINESS ARCHITECTURE BUILDING BLOCKS (BABBS)   320
INFORMATION ARCHITECTURE BUILDING BLOCKS (IABBS)   320
APPLICATION ARCHITECTURE BUILDING BLOCKS (AABBS)   321
TECHNOLOGY ARCHITECTURE BUILDING BLOCKS (TABBS)   321
**IMPORTANCE OF ARCHITECTURE BUILDING BLOCKS IN ENTERPRISE
ARCHITECTURE**   **322**
PROMOTE REUSABILITY AND STANDARDISATION   322
ENSURE CONSISTENT ALIGNMENT WITH STRATEGIC GOALS   323

FACILITATE INTEROPERABILITY AND INTEGRATION 324

SUPPORT SCALABILITY AND FLEXIBILITY 324

IMPROVE QUALITY AND REDUCE RISKS 325

ENABLE EFFICIENT DECISION-MAKING AND GOVERNANCE 325

ACCELERATE TIME-TO-MARKET FOR SOLUTIONS 326

IMPLEMENTING ARCHITECTURE BUILDING BLOCKS IN PRACTICE **326**

STEPS TO IMPLEMENT ABBS IN ENTERPRISE ARCHITECTURE 326

Step 1: Define and Catalogue ABBs 327

Step 2: Align ABBs with Business and IT Strategies 328

Step 3: Develop Guidelines and Standards for ABB Usage 328

Step 4: Map ABBs to Solution Building Blocks (SBBs) 329

Step 5: Integrate ABBs into Solution Development and Delivery

Processes 330

Step 6: Monitor and Evolve ABBs Over Time 331

BEST PRACTICES FOR SUCCESSFUL ABB IMPLEMENTATION **332**

ENSURE STAKEHOLDER ENGAGEMENT 332

MAINTAIN A CENTRALISED REPOSITORY 333

INTEGRATE ABBS INTO EA TOOLING 333

PROMOTE TRAINING AND AWARENESS 334

REGULARLY REVIEW AND UPDATE ABBS 335

MEASURE AND MONITOR USAGE 335

ARCHITECTURE DOCUMENTATION **337**

ARCHITECTURE DOCUMENTATION: THE BACKBONE OF SUCCESSFUL

DEVELOPMENT PROJECTS **339**

KEY ROLES OF ARCHITECTURE DOCUMENTATION 339

Communication Across Stakeholders 339

Validation and Refinement of Architectural Decisions 341

Support for Service/Application Support Teams 341

Foundation for System Understanding and Reuse 342

WHAT TO DOCUMENT **343**

BUSINESS ARCHITECTURE AND PROCESSES 343

Key Elements of Business Architecture and Process Documentation

344

INFORMATION ARCHITECTURE: DATA AND APPLICATION ARCHITECTURE 345

INTEGRATION ARCHITECTURE 347

TECHNICAL ARCHITECTURE 348

ARCHITECTURE DECISION DOCUMENT **349**

IMPORTANCE OF ARCHITECTURE DECISION DOCUMENT 350

Provides Clear Justification for Decisions 350

Enhances Transparency and Accountability 350

Supports Knowledge Management and Continuity 350

Facilitates Impact Analysis and Change Management 351

Promotes Consistent Decision-Making 351

EXAMPLES OF ARCHITECTURE DECISION DOCUMENTS 351

Example 1: Choosing a Cloud Provider 353

Example 2: Selecting a Microservices Architecture Pattern 354

ARCHITECTURE COMPLIANCE CHECKLIST **356**

KEY COMPONENTS OF AN ARCHITECTURE COMPLIANCE CHECKLIST 356

Alignment with Enterprise Architecture Principles and Standards

356

Integration with Existing Systems and Services 357

Consistency Across Architectural Domains 358

Compliance with Regulatory and Security Requirements 358

Use of Approved Technology and Tools 359

Performance, Scalability, and Resilience Requirements 359

Documentation and Artifact Completeness 359

Risk Management and Mitigation 360

Review and Approval Processes 360

Monitoring and Feedback Mechanisms 361

BENEFITS OF USING AN ARCHITECTURE COMPLIANCE CHECKLIST   366

ARCHITECTURE MANAGEMENT AND ENSURING ALIGNMENT   **368**

ENSURE COMPREHENSIVE COVERAGE AND CONSISTENCY ACROSS ARCHITECTURES   368

ESTABLISH LINKS AND REFERENCES AMONG ARCHITECTURE ARTIFACTS   369

MAINTAIN DOCUMENTED ARTEFACTS WITH CROSS-REFERENCES   369

LOAD ARTEFACTS INTO STANDARD TOOLS AND REPOSITORIES   369

ENSURE COMPLIANCE WITH REFERENCE MODELS, METAMODELS, AND STANDARDS   370

DOCUMENT ANY DEVIATIONS OR STEP-OUTS FROM STANDARDS   370

PREPARE FOR ARCHITECTURE REVIEW IN COLLABORATION WITH THE PROJECT MANAGER   371

GOVERNANCE IN ENTERPRISE ARCHITECTURE   **372**

GOVERNANCE STRUCTURE IN ENTERPRISE ARCHITECTURE   **374**

EXECUTIVE STEERING GROUP (ESG)   375

ARCHITECTURE OFFICE   376

PROJECT TEAMS   377

TECHNICAL REVIEW BOARD (TRB)   378

END-TO-END ARCHITECTURE GOVERNANCE PROCESS   **379**

METHOD ADOPTION AND STANDARDS COMPLIANCE   379

CHECKLISTS FOR LIFECYCLE REVIEWS   379

CENTRALISED COMMUNICATION OF STANDARDS   380

ARCHITECTURE & TECHNOLOGY STANDARDS IN EA TOOLING   380

REGULAR REFRESH AND RETIREMENT OF PRINCIPLES   380

MEASURING COMPLIANCE AND PROGRESS   **381**

THE FUTURE OF ENTERPRISE ARCHITECTURE   **382**

AGILITY AND FLEXIBILITY   **383**
EMBRACING AGILE METHODOLOGIES   383
MICROSERVICES AND API-FIRST APPROACHES   384
CLOUD-NATIVE AND HYBRID ARCHITECTURES   384
DIGITAL TRANSFORMATION   **384**
INTEGRATION OF EMERGING TECHNOLOGIES   384
CUSTOMER-CENTRIC DESIGN   385
AUTOMATION AND INTELLIGENT SYSTEMS   385
DATA-CENTRIC ARCHITECTURE   **385**
DATA GOVERNANCE AND MANAGEMENT   385
SCALABLE DATA ARCHITECTURES   386
ADVANCED ANALYTICS AND AI INTEGRATION   386
SECURITY AND COMPLIANCE   **386**
ZERO TRUST ARCHITECTURE   387
PROACTIVE THREAT DETECTION AND RESPONSE   387
COMPLIANCE-DRIVEN ARCHITECTURE   387
SUSTAINABILITY AND GREEN IT   **387**
ENERGY-EFFICIENT DATA CENTRES   388
CLOUD OPTIMISATION AND GREEN COMPUTING   388
SUSTAINABLE SOFTWARE DEVELOPMENT   388

ABOUT THE AUTHOR   **390**

Introduction

Enterprise Architecture is the practice of aligning an organisation's business strategies with its IT infrastructure to achieve business goals. It serves as a blueprint for the organisation's structure and operations, ensuring that the IT infrastructure supports the strategic objectives. Over the years, Enterprise Architecture has evolved from being a purely technical discipline to becoming a vital component of business strategy, helping organisations navigate complex environments and achieve operational excellence.

As mentioned, it is important to keep in mind that Enterprise Architecture is more than just a set of technical diagrams or a collection of IT assets; it is the strategic framework that guides an organisation in aligning its technology landscape with its business goals. This is increasing in importance as organisations are increasingly reliant on technology to drive innovation, streamline operations, and stay competitive. In this aspect, Enterprise Architecture serves as the connective tissue between business strategy and IT infrastructure, ensuring that every technology decision is made with the broader business objectives in mind.

What do Architects do?

Architects play a unique role in shaping environments, both in physical spaces and in digital systems. They are not merely designers or planners; they are observers, interpreters, and creators of patterns that align human behaviour with functional spaces.

Architects as Observers of Behaviour

Architects are, at their core, **observers of behaviour.** Whether working with physical spaces or digital environments, architects must first understand how people interact with their surroundings. They study patterns of behaviour to design spaces or systems that not only meet functional requirements but also support and enhance the way people live, work, and interact. This deep observation is crucial because, as Christopher Alexander, a renowned architect and theorist, notes:

"A place is given its character by certain patterns of events that keep on happening there..."

This observation underlines the idea that environments— whether a city plaza or an enterprise IT system—are defined by recurring patterns of human activity. These patterns are what architects aim to capture, understand, and enhance.

In the context of **IT architecture**, this translates to understanding how users interact with systems, data flows, and digital processes. IT architects must observe how different stakeholders use the technology, where bottlenecks occur, what users find intuitive, and where friction exists. For example, in an e-commerce platform, an architect might observe how customers navigate the site, which features they use most frequently, and where they drop off. These behavioural insights are then used to inform the architecture of the system, ensuring it supports the desired user behaviours and business outcomes.

Creating Space for Patterns of Behaviour to Flourish

With a deep understanding of existing behaviours, architects move on to the next step: **creating space where these patterns of behaviour can happen, flourish, and be generative**. Alexander refers to spaces that are "alive"—where the environment actively supports and encourages the desired behaviours. In IT architecture, this means creating digital spaces—interfaces, workflows, and integrations—that naturally align with how users work and think.

For example, when designing a digital workspace for a remote team, an architect might focus on creating seamless communication flows, easy access to resources, and integrated tools that reflect the team's collaborative behaviours. By designing spaces that accommodate these patterns, architects help create environments that are not just functional but also conducive to growth, creativity, and efficiency.

This approach is not limited to physical space. In enterprise architecture, creating "alive" spaces could mean designing a modular architecture that allows for rapid iteration, experimentation, and continuous improvement—spaces where innovation can flourish without being hampered by rigid structures or silos.

Emergence of a Language of Patterns

From the process of observing behaviours and creating conducive environments, **a language of patterns emerges**. This pattern language represents a set of tried-and-tested solutions to recurring problems within a context. In architecture, whether it is urban planning or software design, these patterns help guide decision-making and ensure coherence and consistency across the entire system.

For example, in software architecture, a common pattern language includes design patterns like "Microservices" for modular architecture, "Singleton" for managing global states, or "Model-View-Controller (MVC)" for separating concerns in user interface development. These patterns have emerged from observing thousands of use cases and refining the solutions over time.

By employing a pattern language, architects are not starting from scratch for every project; instead, they are expanding an existing vocabulary. This allows for endless possibilities of creation, as these patterns can be combined, modified, and adapted to meet specific needs. The more extensive and refined the pattern language, the more tools an architect has at their disposal to solve complex problems creatively.

Expanding the Vocabulary of Pattern Language in IT Architecture

In IT architecture, architects play a crucial role in **expanding the pattern language** for their customers or stakeholders. This involves not just applying existing patterns but also creating new ones that better fit the unique needs and contexts of the organisation. By expanding the vocabulary of patterns, architects help organisations grow their capabilities, innovate more effectively, and respond to changing environments.

For instance, an IT architect working with a healthcare provider might notice a recurring need for secure, real-time data sharing between different departments. While traditional patterns might suggest point-to-point integrations or batch processing, the architect might introduce new patterns, such as an API gateway combined with event-driven architecture, to facilitate more dynamic and secure data flows. By doing so, they expand the organisation's vocabulary and enable it to meet its evolving needs more effectively.

The Importance of Enterprise Architecture

In today's rapidly changing business environment, organisations face numerous challenges, from digital disruption and regulatory compliance to globalisation and the demand for greater operational efficiency. These challenges require organisations to be agile, responsive, and innovative. However, achieving this level of agility and innovation is impossible without a well-structured approach to managing the complex web of technologies, processes, and information flows that underpin the modern enterprise.

This is where Enterprise Architecture comes into play. Enterprise Architecture provides a holistic view of the organisation, mapping out the relationships between business processes, information systems, technology infrastructure, and data. By doing so, it helps organisations identify redundancies, streamline operations, and ensure that all components of the enterprise are working together harmoniously to achieve strategic objectives.

The Evolution of Enterprise Architecture

The concept of Enterprise Architecture has evolved significantly since its inception in the 1980s. Initially, Enterprise Architecture was primarily concerned with IT alignment—ensuring that the IT infrastructure supported business operations. However, as organisations became more complex and technology began to play a more central role in business strategy, the scope of Enterprise Architecture has expanded.

Today, Enterprise Architecture encompasses not just IT, but also business processes, data management, security, and even organisational culture. It is a multidisciplinary practice that requires collaboration across various departments, from IT and operations to finance and marketing. The modern Enterprise Architect must be both a technologist and a strategist, capable of understanding the nuances of business strategy while also possessing deep technical expertise.

The Strategic Role of Enterprise Architecture

As mentioned, one of the key functions of Enterprise Architecture is to bridge the gap between business strategy and IT execution. In many organisations, there is often a disconnect between the strategic goals set by leadership and the day-to-day operations carried out by IT and other departments. This disconnect can lead to misaligned priorities, inefficient processes, and ultimately, a failure to achieve business objectives.

Enterprise Architecture addresses this issue by providing a structured approach to aligning business and IT. It ensures that every technology investment is made with the broader business strategy in mind, and that IT initiatives are designed to support the organisation's long-term goals. By providing a clear roadmap for technology implementation, Enterprise Architecture helps organisations avoid costly mistakes and ensures that they are able to quickly adapt to changes in the business environment.

The Value of Enterprise Architecture in Decision-Making

In addition to its role in aligning business and IT, Enterprise Architecture also plays a critical role in decision-making. In our complex and interconnected world, organisations are faced with a myriad of choices when it comes to technology adoption, process optimisation, and business model innovation. Enterprise Architecture provides the framework for making informed decisions by offering a comprehensive view of the organisation's current state, as well as a blueprint for its future state.

This holistic perspective allows organisations to assess the potential impact of different decisions on various parts of the enterprise, ensuring that decisions are made in a way that maximises value and minimises risk. Whether it's deciding which technologies to invest in, how to optimise business processes, or how to structure the organisation for future growth, Enterprise Architecture provides the insights needed to make strategic, informed choices.

The Future of Enterprise Architecture

As we move further into the digital age, the role of Enterprise Architecture is set to become even more critical. With the rise of digital transformation, cloud computing, artificial intelligence, and other emerging technologies, organisations will need to be more agile and adaptable than ever before. Enterprise Architecture will play a central role in guiding organisations through this transformation, helping them navigate the complexities of the digital landscape while ensuring that their technology investments are aligned with their long-term business goals.

Moreover, as the business environment continues to evolve, so too will the practice of Enterprise Architecture. We can expect to see new frameworks, methodologies, and tools emerge, designed to help organisations manage the increasing complexity of their operations and technology landscapes. The future of Enterprise Architecture will be characterised by a greater emphasis on agility, flexibility, and innovation, as organisations seek to remain competitive in an ever-changing world. We would discuss this more at the end of this book.

Evolution of Enterprise Architecture

The Origins of Enterprise Architecture

The roots of Enterprise Architecture can be traced back to the 1980s, a time when businesses began to recognise the growing complexity of their IT systems and the need for a more structured approach to managing these assets. The rapid proliferation of computing technologies, combined with the increasing reliance on IT to support business operations, highlighted the challenges of ensuring that technology investments were aligned with business objectives. This period marked the beginning of what would become the discipline of Enterprise Architecture.

One of the foundational moments in the history of Enterprise Architecture was the introduction of the Zachman Framework by John Zachman in 1987. Zachman, then an IBM employee, observed that the traditional approaches to system development were inadequate for managing the complexity of modern enterprises. He proposed a framework that would help organisations map out their IT systems in a more structured and coherent manner. The Zachman Framework was revolutionary in that it provided a way to organise and understand the various components of an enterprise, including data, processes, networks, and systems.

The Zachman Framework laid the groundwork for what would become Enterprise Architecture by emphasising the importance of having a comprehensive, holistic view of the organisation. It introduced the concept of different perspectives, or views, on the architecture, such as the planner's view, the designer's view, and the implementer's view, each addressing different aspects of the enterprise. This multi-dimensional approach allowed organisations to better manage the complexity of their IT systems and align them more effectively with their business needs.

The Evolution of Enterprise Architecture in the 1990s

The 1990s saw the formalisation and expansion of Enterprise Architecture as a discipline. During this decade, several key developments helped shape the practice of Enterprise Architecture and establish it as a critical function within organisations.

One of the most significant developments was the introduction of The Open Group Architecture Framework (TOGAF) in the mid-1990s. TOGAF was initially developed by The Open Group as a methodology for developing and managing enterprise architectures. Unlike the Zachman Framework, which was more focused on providing a classification scheme, TOGAF provided a step-by-step process for designing, implementing, and maintaining an enterprise architecture.

TOGAF's Architecture Development Method (ADM) became a cornerstone of Enterprise Architecture practices, offering a structured approach to architecture development that could be adapted to the specific needs of different organisations. It introduced concepts such as the architecture vision, business architecture, information systems architecture, technology architecture, and opportunities and solutions, providing a comprehensive methodology for managing the entire architecture lifecycle.

Another important development during this period was the recognition of Enterprise Architecture's strategic role within organisations. As businesses became more reliant on technology to drive competitive advantage, it became clear that Enterprise Architecture was not just an IT function but a key enabler of business strategy. Organisations began to see Enterprise Architecture as a way to ensure that their IT investments were aligned with their long-term goals, helping them to optimise their operations, reduce costs, and innovate more effectively.

The Rise of Government and Industry-Specific Frameworks

The late 1990s and early 2000s saw the emergence of government and industry-specific Enterprise Architecture frameworks, reflecting the growing importance of Enterprise Architecture across different sectors. One of the most notable of these was the Federal Enterprise Architecture Framework (FEAF), developed by the U.S. federal government.

FEAF was designed to help federal agencies manage their IT resources more effectively and ensure that their IT systems were interoperable and aligned with their missions. It provided a standardised approach to Enterprise Architecture, with a focus on ensuring that government agencies could work together more effectively and share information across different departments. FEAF also emphasised the importance of security and compliance, reflecting the unique needs of government organisations.

Another significant development during this period was the introduction of the Department of Defence Architecture Framework (DoDAF) and the Ministry of Defence Architecture Framework (MoDAF) in the United Kingdom. These frameworks were developed to address the specific needs of defence organisations, which required highly structured and secure architectures to support their complex operations. DoDAF and MoDAF provided detailed guidelines for designing and managing architectures in a defence context, with a focus on ensuring interoperability, security, and resilience.

The emergence of these industry-specific frameworks highlighted the growing recognition of Enterprise Architecture as a critical function across different sectors. It also underscored the need for organisations to tailor their Enterprise Architecture practices to meet their specific needs and challenges.

The Expansion of Enterprise Architecture in the 2000s

The 2000s marked a period of significant growth and expansion for Enterprise Architecture. During this decade, Enterprise Architecture became more widely adopted across a range of industries, as organisations recognised the value of having a structured approach to managing their IT and business processes.

One of the key trends during this period was the increasing focus on business-IT alignment. Organisations began to see Enterprise Architecture as a way to bridge the gap between their business strategy and their IT infrastructure, ensuring that their technology investments were directly supporting their business goals. This shift in focus was reflected in the development of new Enterprise Architecture frameworks and methodologies that emphasised the importance of aligning IT with business strategy.

For example, Gartner introduced its own approach to Enterprise Architecture, which focused on the concept of "business outcome-driven Enterprise Architecture." This approach emphasised the need for Enterprise Architecture to be directly linked to business outcomes, rather than being a purely technical function. Gartner's framework encouraged organisations to use Enterprise Architecture as a tool for driving business change and innovation, rather than just managing IT assets.

16

The 2000s also saw the rise of service-oriented architecture (SOA), a design principle that emphasised the importance of building flexible, modular IT systems that could be easily adapted to changing business needs. SOA was closely aligned with the principles of Enterprise Architecture, as it provided a way to design IT systems that were more responsive to business requirements. Many organisations began to integrate SOA principles into their Enterprise Architecture practices, leading to more agile and adaptable architectures.

The Impact of Digital Transformation

The 2010s ushered in the era of digital transformation, a period marked by the rapid adoption of new technologies such as cloud computing, big data, artificial intelligence, and the Internet of Things (IoT). These technologies brought new opportunities for innovation, but also new challenges for managing the complexity of modern enterprises. As organisations embraced digital transformation, the role of Enterprise Architecture became even more critical.

During this period, Enterprise Architecture evolved to address the demands of digital transformation. Traditional Enterprise Architecture practices, which had focused on managing IT assets and aligning them with business processes, were no longer sufficient in the face of rapid technological change.

17

Organisations needed to become more agile and responsive, and Enterprise Architecture had to evolve to support this need.

One of the key developments during this period was the shift towards "lean" and "agile" Enterprise Architecture practices. Lean Enterprise Architecture emphasised the need to eliminate waste and focus on delivering value to the organisation, while agile Enterprise Architecture promoted iterative, incremental approaches to architecture development. These new approaches allowed organisations to respond more quickly to changing business needs and take advantage of new technologies as they emerged.

Another significant trend was the increasing emphasis on data-centric architecture. As data became a key strategic asset, organisations recognised the need for Enterprise Architecture to focus more on data management and governance. This led to the development of new Enterprise Architecture practices that prioritised the design of data architectures capable of handling large volumes of data, ensuring data quality, and supporting advanced analytics.

The Future of Enterprise Architecture

As we look to the future, it is clear that Enterprise Architecture will continue to evolve in response to emerging trends and technologies. The rise of artificial intelligence, machine learning, and automation will bring new opportunities for innovation, but also new challenges for managing the complexity of enterprise architectures. Organisations will need to continue adapting their Enterprise Architecture practices to keep pace with these changes.

One of the key trends shaping the future of Enterprise Architecture is the increasing focus on agility and flexibility. In a rapidly changing business environment, organisations need to be able to quickly adapt to new opportunities and challenges. This will require Enterprise Architecture practices that are more dynamic and responsive, capable of evolving in real-time as the organisation's needs change.

Another important trend is the growing importance of sustainability and green IT. As organisations become more aware of their environmental impact, there will be a greater emphasis on designing architectures that are energy-efficient and environmentally friendly. Enterprise Architecture will play a key role in helping organisations achieve their sustainability goals by designing IT systems that minimise energy consumption and reduce waste.

Some Enterprise Architecture Frameworks

There are several Enterprise Architecture frameworks that organisations can use to guide their architecture practices. Each framework has its own strengths and is suited to different types of organisations. I will introduce the following frameworks in detail in this book. The frameworks that will be discussed are as follows:

The Zachman Framework

One of the earliest Enterprise Architecture frameworks, it focuses on defining the components of an organisation and their relationships in a structured manner. It is highly detailed and suitable for organisations that require a comprehensive understanding of their architecture.

The Open Group Architecture Framework (TOGAF)

TOGAF is one of the most widely used Enterprise Architecture frameworks. It provides a detailed methodology for developing, implementing, and maintaining an Enterprise Architecture. TOGAF is flexible and adaptable, making it suitable for organisations of all sizes and industries.

Federal Enterprise Architecture Framework (FEAF)

Developed by the U.S. federal government, FEAF is designed for large, government-related organisations. It emphasises standardisation and interoperability, making it ideal for complex, multi-agency environments.

Gartner's Enterprise Architecture Framework

This framework focuses on aligning IT with business strategy and is more business-oriented than other frameworks. It emphasises the role of Enterprise Architecture in driving business outcomes and managing change.

The Ministry of Defence Architecture Framework (MoDAF)

Initially developed for defence organisations, MoDAF has been adapted for use in other sectors as well. It is highly structured and focuses on meeting specific organisational requirements.

The Dragon1 Framework

The Dragon1 Framework is a relatively newer and innovative approach to Enterprise Architecture, developed in the Netherlands. It is both a framework and a method, designed to help organisations visualise, manage, and improve their enterprise architecture in a way that supports strategic decision-making and drives business transformation.

The Zachman Framework

The Zachman Framework, introduced by John Zachman in 1987, is one of the most seminal and enduring contributions to the field of Enterprise Architecture. It is not a methodology in the traditional sense, but rather a taxonomy—a structured way of viewing and understanding the complex interrelationships within an enterprise. The framework is designed to provide a comprehensive, organised way of describing an enterprise's architecture, ensuring that all aspects are covered and understood from multiple perspectives.

History of the Zachman Framework

John Zachman, an experienced systems analyst and a practitioner at IBM, began developing the ideas that would lead to the Zachman Framework during his tenure at the company. In the early 1980s, Zachman observed that as organisations grew, their IT systems became increasingly complex and fragmented. This fragmentation often led to misalignment between IT capabilities and business objectives, resulting in inefficiencies, increased costs, and reduced organisational agility.

Zachman recognised the need for a comprehensive, structured approach to managing these complexities—a way to ensure that all aspects of an organisation's systems were properly aligned with its business processes and strategic goals. His work drew upon principles from other fields, particularly architecture and engineering, where the use of frameworks and structured models was already well established.

The Zachman Framework is based on the premise that the same complex system can be described in different ways depending on the stakeholder's perspective. By categorising these perspectives and the different elements of the system, the framework allows organisations to ensure that all necessary aspects are considered when planning, developing, and managing enterprise architecture.

Audience Perspective (Classification Names)	What	How	Where	Who	When	Why	Model Names (Classification Names)
Planner Perspective	Inventory Identification	Process Identification	Distribution Identification	Responsibility Identification	Timing Identification	Motivation Identification	Scope Context
Owner Perspective	Inventory Definition	Process Definition	Distribution Definition	Responsibility Definition	Timing Definition	Motivation Definition	Business Concepts
Designer Perspective	Inventory Representation	Process Representation	Distribution Representation	Responsibility Representation	Timing Representation	Motivation Representation	System Logic
Builder Perspective	Inventory Specification	Process Specification	Distribution Specification	Responsibility Specification	Timing Specification	Motivation Specification	Technology Physics
Subcontractor Perspective	Inventory Configuration	Process Configuration	Distribution Configuration	Responsibility Configuration	Timing Configuration	Motivation Configuration	Tools Components
Enterprise Perspective	Inventory Instantiations	Process Instantiations	Distribution Instantiations	Responsibility Instantiations	Timing Instantiations	Motivation Instantiations	Operation Instances
Audience Perspective (Enterprise Names)	Inventory Sets	Process Flows	Distribution Networks	Responsibility Assignment	Timing Cycles	Motivation Intentions	Model Names (Enterprise Names)

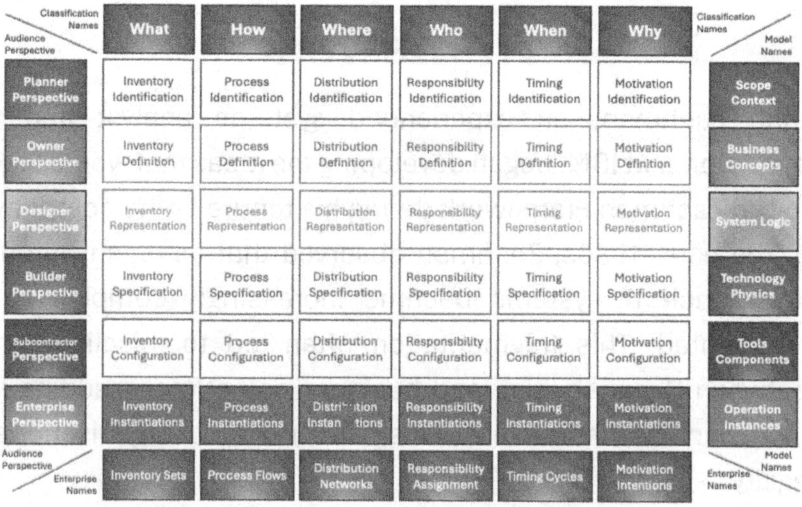

Figure 1:The Zachman Framework for Enterprise Architecture v3.0

Structure of the Zachman Framework

The Zachman Framework is structured as a two-dimensional matrix. The columns represent different aspects or dimensions of the architecture, while the rows represent different perspectives or viewpoints of the stakeholders involved in the enterprise. This matrix provides a way to categorise and relate the various artifacts, models, and documentation used to describe an enterprise's architecture.

The Column - Architectural Aspects

The columns of the Zachman Framework represent different aspects of the architecture that must be addressed:

What (Data): This column addresses the data or information aspect of the enterprise. It focuses on what the organisation needs to know to operate, encompassing data models, data structures, and information systems.

How (Function): This column represents the functional aspects of the enterprise, including processes, functions, and workflows. It defines how the enterprise operates, including the steps, procedures, and methodologies used to accomplish tasks.

Where (Network): This column deals with the geographical distribution of the enterprise's operations. It includes the locations of business activities, the distribution of resources,

25

and the connectivity between these locations, addressing how the enterprise's operations are geographically organised.

Who (People): This column focuses on the people or organisational aspect, addressing who is involved in the operations of the enterprise. It includes roles, responsibilities, organisational structures, and human resources.

When (Time): This column represents the timing aspects of the enterprise, addressing when events and processes occur. It includes schedules, timelines, events, and temporal dependencies.

Why (Motivation): This column covers the motivational aspects, addressing why the enterprise operates as it does. It includes goals, strategies, business objectives, and the rationale behind decisions and processes.

The Rows - Stakeholder Perspectives

The rows of the Zachman Framework represent different perspectives or viewpoints of stakeholders within the enterprise. Each perspective is associated with a different level of detail, from the broadest conceptual view to the most detailed, implementation-specific view:

Planner (Scope Contexts): The planner's perspective represents the highest level of abstraction, focusing on the scope and context of the enterprise. This row provides an overview of the business's goals, purpose, and environment, outlining the general strategy and boundaries without delving into detailed specifications.

Owner (Business Concepts): The owner's perspective focuses on the business view, detailing what the business needs to achieve its objectives. This row describes the business's processes, data requirements, organisational structure, and other business-centric elements, often captured in business models and high-level requirements.

Designer (System Logic): The designer's perspective translates the business requirements into system-level designs. This row addresses how the business needs will be fulfilled by IT systems, encompassing logical data models, system architectures, and software design without yet considering the specifics of technology.

Builder (Technology Physics): The builder's perspective focuses on the implementation details, translating the system designs into specific technology implementations. This row deals with physical data models, network architectures, and technical specifications, including hardware, software, and network components.

Subcontractor (Detailed Representations): The subcontractor's perspective involves the detailed specifications required to build and assemble the components of the architecture. This row covers the detailed design documents, code, configurations, and other granular specifications needed for construction and assembly.

Enterprise (Functioning Systems): The final perspective represents the functioning enterprise, where all elements come together to form a working system. This row focuses on the operational enterprise, where all plans, designs, and implementations are realised and functioning together.

How the Zachman Framework is Used

The Zachman Framework serves as a comprehensive checklist for Enterprise Architecture, ensuring that all relevant aspects of the enterprise are considered from each stakeholder's perspective. It helps organisations to:

Identify and Address Gaps: By examining each cell in the framework, organisations can identify gaps or missing elements in their architecture, ensuring that all necessary aspects are considered.

Improve Communication: The framework provides a common language and structure that can be used to improve communication among stakeholders with different perspectives and levels of detail.

Align Business and IT: The framework helps to ensure that business needs are properly translated into IT requirements and that IT implementations are aligned with business goals.

Manage Complexity: By breaking down the architecture into manageable components, the framework helps organisations to manage the complexity of their enterprise and ensure that all aspects are properly integrated.

Support Decision-Making: The framework provides a structured approach to documenting and understanding the enterprise, supporting informed decision-making at all levels.

Examples of Using the Zachman Framework

Example 1: Data Management

When dealing with a data management system, the artefacts that are requirement to be developed using the Zachman Framework would be as follows:

What (Data) Perspective:

Planner: High-level overview of data requirements.

This is the most abstract level, where the focus is on the broad, strategic view of the organisation's data needs.

The Planner's perspective is concerned with identifying what types of data are necessary for the organisation to function effectively. At this level, the details are minimal; the focus is on understanding the scope of data required to support the business's strategic goals. This might involve identifying categories of data, such as customer information, financial records, or product inventories, without going into the specifics of how this data is structured or managed.

For example, a retail company might determine that it needs data on customer demographics, sales transactions, inventory levels, and supplier information. The Planner would outline these broad categories as essential data types for running the business.

Owner: Business data models that define key entities and relationships.

The Owner's perspective is concerned with the business view of data, focusing on how the business interacts with and utilises data.

At this level, the business data models are developed. These models define key business entities (such as customers, products, and transactions) and the relationships between them. The focus is on how data supports business processes and operations. The models created here help in understanding how data flows within the business and how different data entities are interconnected.

Following the example above, the retail company might create a business data model that defines entities like "Customer," "Order," "Product," and "Supplier." The model would detail how a customer places an order, how products are linked to orders, and how suppliers are related to products.

Designer: Logical data models detailing attributes and relationships.

The Designer's perspective focuses on translating the business requirements into a logical data model that defines how data will be structured logically, without considering physical storage.

At this level, the logical data models are created. These models provide more detail than the business data models, specifying attributes (such as customer names, product descriptions, and order dates) and the relationships between different data entities. The logical data model is still independent of any particular technology or database system; it's a conceptual blueprint for how data should be organised.

Again, following the example, the retail company might create a logical data model where the "Customer" entity includes attributes like "CustomerID", "Name", "Email", and "Address". The "Order" entity might include "OrderID", "OrderDate", and "TotalAmount" and these entities would be related by a "CustomerID" foreign key in the "Order" entity.

Builder: Physical data models specifying how data is stored in databases.

The Builder's perspective is about turning the logical data models into physical data models that detail how data will be stored in actual database systems.

This level involves designing the physical data model, which specifies how data will be physically stored in databases. It includes decisions about database tables, columns, indexes, data types, and storage formats. The physical model is tailored to the specific database management system (DBMS) being used and considers performance, storage efficiency, and access speed.

Going deeper with the retail company example, the physical data model might define a table in a SQL database for the "Customer" entity with columns for "CustomerID" (as an integer), "Name" (as a varchar), "Email" (as a varchar), and so on. The "Order" table would similarly be defined with the appropriate data types and indexing for efficient queries.

Subcontractor: Detailed database schemas and code for database management.

The Subcontractor's perspective involves the detailed technical specifications and implementation aspects.

At this level, the focus is on the creation of detailed database schemas and the necessary code for database management. This includes writing the SQL code to create tables, defining relationships, constraints, indexes, and possibly creating stored procedures or triggers to manage the data. The Subcontractor's work ensures that the data is structured and managed according to the specifications laid out in the physical data model.

Following on, the retail company's database administrator or developer might write SQL scripts to create the "Customer" and "Order" tables in the database, including constraints like primary keys and foreign keys, and create indexes on frequently queried columns. They might also develop stored procedures for common operations like inserting a new order or updating customer information.

Enterprise: Operational databases running live data.

The Enterprise perspective represents the final, operational view of the data management process, where the system is live and in use.

This is the level at which all previous planning, designing, and building come together to form a functioning system. The operational databases are now running and actively used in the organisation's day-to-day operations. Data is being collected, stored, retrieved, and managed in real-time, supporting the business processes.

In the case of the retail company example, the operational database would be in use, with customers placing orders online or in stores, and the system processing and storing this information in real-time. The database is queried to generate reports, manage inventory, and track sales, enabling the business to operate efficiently.

Example 2: Process Automation

Let's show another example when applied to process or workflow architecture. Ibn this case we will explore the artefacts that are requirement to be developed using the Zachman Framework for process automation.

How (Function) Perspective:

Planner: Overview of key business processes and workflows.

As before, the Planner's perspective is the most abstract and strategic view, focusing on the overall scope of the organisation's functions and workflows.

At this level, the Planner identifies and outlines the key business processes and workflows that the organisation relies on to operate effectively. This overview is high-level, focusing on the main functions and how they interconnect, without going into detailed specifics. The Planner's job is to ensure that all critical business processes are accounted for and that they align with the organisation's strategic objectives.

In the retail company example, the Planner might outline the key processes such as "Order Fulfilment", "Inventory Management", "Customer Service" and "Supplier Coordination". These processes would be identified as essential for the company's operations, and their high-level flow would be mapped out, showing how they interact with one another.

Owner: Detailed process models that describe business operations.

The Owner's perspective dives deeper into the business operations, focusing on how each key process functions in detail.

At this level, the Owner creates detailed process models that describe the specific steps involved in each business operation. These models include the sequence of tasks, the roles involved, and the decision points. The goal is to fully document how the business operates, ensuring that all necessary activities are captured and understood.

For the "Order Fulfilment" process, the Owner might create a detailed flowchart showing the steps from receiving an order, checking inventory, processing payment, packaging the product, and shipping it to the customer. Each step would be detailed, including who is responsible for it and any decisions that need to be made along the way (e.g., what happens if an item is out of stock).

Designer: System workflows that automate business processes.

The Designer's perspective focuses on translating the detailed business processes into system workflows that can be automated.

At this level, the Designer develops system workflows that replicate the business processes in an automated fashion. This involves creating workflows within software systems that can execute the business processes without manual intervention. The Designer ensures that these workflows align with the business process models and can effectively support the business operations.

With the retail example, The Designer might create an automated workflow in an enterprise resource planning (ERP) system that handles the entire "Order Fulfilment" process. This system workflow would automatically move an order through each step—checking inventory, processing payment, updating stock levels, and triggering the shipping process—all based on the detailed process model created by the Owner.

Builder: Technical workflows implemented in software tools.

The Builder's perspective is concerned with the technical implementation of the workflows designed by the Designer.

At this level, the Builder takes the system workflows and implements them using specific software tools and technologies. This involves configuring the software, setting up automation rules, and integrating various systems to ensure that the workflows function correctly within the technical environment. The Builder's role is to make sure that the workflows are operationally ready and can be executed by the software.

Following the retail example, the Builder might configure the ERP system to handle order processing by setting up automation scripts, integrating the payment gateway, and ensuring that inventory levels are updated in real-time. They might also configure notifications or triggers that alert staff when an order is delayed or when there's a problem in the process.

Subcontractor: Detailed software code and configuration for workflow automation.

The Subcontractor's perspective involves the detailed, technical work required to implement the automation.

At this level, the Subcontractor writes the specific code and configurations necessary to automate the workflows within the chosen software tools. This includes programming scripts, developing custom software components, configuring APIs for system integration, and setting up the necessary databases. The work here is very detailed and technical, ensuring that the automation is robust, reliable, and scalable.

Going further with the example, the Subcontractor might write custom code to integrate the ERP system with the warehouse management system (WMS) to automate inventory updates. They could also develop scripts that automatically generate shipping labels or send confirmation emails to customers when their orders are dispatched.

Enterprise: Fully automated business processes running in production.

The Enterprise perspective represents the final, operational view where the automated processes are live and in use.

At this level, the processes are fully automated and operational within the organisation. The automation is running in a live environment, executing the business processes as designed and implemented. The enterprise benefits from improved efficiency, reduced manual intervention, and faster process execution.

In the retail company, the fully automated "Order Fulfilment" process would now be running in production. Customers place orders online, and the system automatically processes the orders, updates inventory, processes payments, and manages shipping—all without manual intervention. The company might see faster order processing times, fewer errors, and improved customer satisfaction as a result of the automation.

The two examples illustrate how the Zachman Framework guides the development and management of data and process in an enterprise by breaking down the process into six levels, each corresponding to a different stakeholder's perspective. From the high-level strategic overview to the detailed implementation and operational use, the framework ensures that data management and process automation are comprehensive, aligned with business needs, and technically sound. This structured approach helps in systematically addressing all aspects of transformation work ensuring that the organisation's approach is robust, efficient, and capable of supporting its business goals.

Strengths of the Zachman Framework

The Zachman Framework is widely recognised for its robust and comprehensive approach to Enterprise Architecture (EA). It has several key strengths that have contributed to its enduring relevance in the field:

Comprehensive Coverage Across Multiple Dimensions

One of the most significant strengths of the Zachman Framework is its ability to provide comprehensive coverage of an enterprise's architecture across multiple dimensions. By structuring the architecture into different columns (What, How, Where, Who, When, Why) and rows (Planner, Owner, Designer, Builder, Subcontractor, Enterprise), the framework ensures that all aspects of the organisation are considered. This structured approach prevents oversight, ensuring that nothing critical is missed when designing or analysing an architecture. It facilitates a holistic view of the enterprise, covering everything from strategic goals to detailed technical implementations.

Versatility Across Industries and Organisations

The Zachman Framework is highly versatile and can be applied across a wide range of industries and organisations, regardless of size or complexity. Its abstract nature allows it to be tailored to the specific needs of different organisations, making it relevant whether it's being used in government agencies, financial institutions, healthcare, or manufacturing. This adaptability is a major strength, as it allows the framework to be useful in diverse contexts, from large multinational corporations to small businesses.

Improved Communication and Collaboration

By providing a common language and structure for describing enterprise architecture, the Zachman Framework significantly enhances communication and collaboration among stakeholders. It breaks down the architecture into manageable, understandable components that can be communicated effectively across different departments and levels of the organisation. This common understanding helps bridge the gap between business and IT, ensuring that both sides are aligned and working towards the same goals. It also fosters better collaboration between architects, designers, builders, and end-users by providing clarity on their respective roles and contributions.

Alignment of Business and IT

The framework's multi-dimensional approach ensures that IT systems and infrastructures are aligned with business strategies and goals. By mapping out different perspectives (from high-level business goals to detailed IT systems), the Zachman Framework helps ensure that every technological decision made within an organisation is done with the broader business objectives in mind. This alignment is crucial for maximising the value of IT investments and ensuring that the organisation's technology supports and drives its strategic goals.

Management of Complexity

The Zachman Framework excels at managing the complexity inherent in large organisations. By breaking down the architecture into distinct perspectives and dimensions, the framework makes it easier to handle the complexity of large-scale IT systems and business processes. This structured approach allows organisations to systematically address the various aspects of their architecture, making it easier to manage and evolve over time. It provides a clear roadmap for understanding how different parts of the organisation fit together and how changes in one area might impact others.

Limitations of the Zachman Framework

Despite its strengths, the Zachman Framework is not without its limitations. Some of these challenges can make it difficult to apply effectively in certain contexts:

Complexity and Difficulty in Implementation

The very comprehensiveness that makes the Zachman Framework powerful can also make it complex and difficult to implement, especially for organisations that are new to Enterprise Architecture. The framework's detailed structure requires a significant amount of time and effort to fully understand and apply. Organisations may struggle with the level of detail and the number of perspectives that need to be addressed, leading to potential confusion and inefficiencies. This complexity can be particularly challenging for smaller organisations or those with limited resources, as they may not have the capacity to fully engage with the framework's demands.

Lack of Prescriptive Guidance

The Zachman Framework is more of a taxonomy or classification scheme than a step-by-step methodology. While it provides a structured way to categorise and view the various elements of an enterprise, it does not prescribe specific methods or processes for how to develop or implement the architecture. This lack of prescriptive guidance can be a limitation for organisations seeking concrete steps and actionable processes to follow. Without a clear methodology, organisations may find it challenging to move from theory to practice, leading to potential gaps between architectural planning and execution.

Static Nature and Difficulty in Adaptation

The Zachman Framework is often criticised for its static nature. It provides a snapshot of the enterprise architecture at a given point in time but does not inherently account for the dynamic changes that occur within an organisation. In fast-paced environments where businesses need to quickly adapt to new technologies, market conditions, or regulatory requirements, the static nature of the Zachman Framework can be a hindrance. Organisations may find it difficult to adapt the framework to evolving needs without significant customisation or augmentation with other methodologies.

Tool-Agnostic Nature

While the tool-agnostic nature of the Zachman Framework can be seen as a strength, allowing it to be applied across different contexts, it can also be a limitation. The framework does not provide specific tools, software, or techniques for implementation, leaving organisations to find or develop their own tools to support the architecture process. This can be a barrier to adoption, particularly for organisations that do not have the expertise or resources to develop custom solutions. Without the right tools, applying the framework effectively can be challenging and may lead to inconsistent results.

Potential for Over-Documentation

The detailed and comprehensive nature of the Zachman Framework can lead to a tendency for over-documentation. Organisations may feel compelled to fill out every cell in the framework, even when some aspects may not be relevant or necessary for their specific context. This can result in excessive documentation that is time-consuming to produce and maintain, without necessarily providing proportional value. Over-documentation can also create challenges in keeping the architecture up to date, as changes in one area might require updates across multiple perspectives.

Misalignment with Agile and Lean Practices

The Zachman Framework, with its emphasis on comprehensive documentation and detailed planning, may not align well with Agile and Lean practices that prioritise flexibility, rapid iteration, and minimal viable documentation. Organisations that are deeply invested in Agile methodologies may find the Zachman Framework too rigid and cumbersome for their needs. The framework's traditional approach to architecture, with its focus on detailed planning upfront, can be at odds with the iterative and incremental nature of Agile development, potentially leading to conflicts in implementation.

The Zachman Framework remains one of the most influential and widely recognised frameworks in the field of Enterprise Architecture. Its strengths lie in its comprehensive coverage, versatility, and ability to align business and IT, making it a powerful tool for managing complexity and improving communication across an organisation. However, its complexity, lack of prescriptive guidance, and static nature can present challenges, particularly for organisations that are new to Enterprise Architecture or those operating in fast-paced, dynamic environments. While the Zachman Framework provides a solid foundation for understanding and organising enterprise architecture, it is important for organisations to be aware of its limitations and consider how it can be complemented with other methodologies or tools to meet their specific needs.

The Open Group
Architecture Framework
(TOGAF)

$$TOGAF^®$$

TOGAF, or The Open Group Architecture Framework, is one of the most widely recognised and used frameworks in the field of Enterprise Architecture. It was developed by The Open Group, a global consortium that seeks to enable the achievement of business objectives through open standards and frameworks.

History of TOGAF

The origins of TOGAF can be traced back to the late 1980s and early 1990s, during a period when organisations were increasingly recognising the need for a structured approach to managing their IT architectures. The U.S. Department of Defence (DoD) was among the pioneers in this area, developing a framework known as the Technical Architecture

Framework for Information Management (TAFIM). TAFIM was designed to provide a standard approach to IT architecture that could support the development of interoperable systems within the DoD.

Recognising the potential for broader application, The Open Group adapted and expanded upon TAFIM to create the first version of TOGAF, which was released in 1995. Since then, TOGAF has undergone several iterations, with each new version incorporating feedback from practitioners and addressing emerging trends in technology and business. TOGAF 10, launched on 25 April 2022, is currently the latest version as of 2024, represents a mature and comprehensive framework that continues to evolve with the changing needs of organisations worldwide.

How TOGAF is Used for Enterprise Architecture

TOGAF provides a detailed methodology and set of tools for developing, managing, and governing an enterprise architecture. It is particularly well-suited for large organisations that need to align their IT strategy with their business goals, manage complexity, and drive transformation initiatives. TOGAF is used in a variety of ways across different industries, often tailored to meet the specific needs of the organisation.

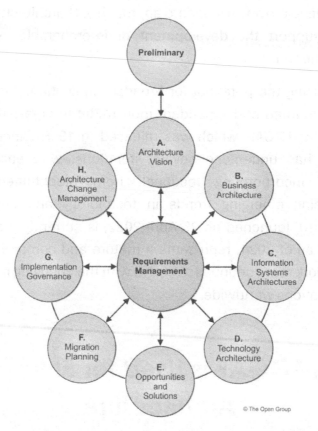

Figure 2: TOGAF 10 (image from the Open Group website)

The Architecture Development Method (ADM)

At the core of TOGAF is the Architecture Development Method (ADM), a step-by-step approach that guides architects through the process of developing and managing an enterprise architecture. The ADM is a flexible, iterative method that can be adapted to suit the unique requirements of different organisations. It is organised into several phases:

Preliminary Phase: In this phase, the groundwork for the architecture effort is established. This includes defining the scope, identifying stakeholders, and securing organisational commitment. The Preliminary Phase also involves setting up the architecture framework, including principles, governance structures, and tools.

Phase A - Architecture Vision: This phase involves creating a high-level vision of the architecture, aligned with business goals and stakeholder needs. It sets the direction for the architecture project and defines the scope of the architecture work.

Phases B, C, and D - Business, Information Systems, and Technology Architecture: These phases involve the detailed design of the architecture across three domains: business architecture (Phase B), data and application architecture (Phase C), and technology architecture (Phase D). Each phase focuses on specific aspects of the architecture, ensuring that all necessary components are addressed.

Phase E - Opportunities and Solutions: This phase involves identifying opportunities for improvement and developing solutions to address them. It focuses on how to implement the architecture, including identifying gaps between the current and target architectures.

Phase F - Migration Planning: In this phase, the focus is on developing a roadmap for migrating from the current architecture to the target architecture. It includes planning the implementation of the architecture in phases, managing risks, and securing necessary resources.

Phase G - Implementation Governance: This phase involves overseeing the implementation of the architecture, ensuring that it is carried out according to plan and that any deviations are managed effectively.

Phase H - Architecture Change Management: The final phase focuses on managing changes to the architecture over time. It ensures that the architecture remains aligned with business goals and is updated as needed to reflect changes in the organisation or its environment.

Requirements Management: This is a continuous process throughout the ADM, ensuring that the architecture remains aligned with business requirements and stakeholder needs.

TOGAF's Architecture Content Framework

TOGAF also includes an Architecture Content Framework, which provides a structured approach for creating architectural artifacts. These artifacts include models, views, and other documents that describe the architecture and support decision-making. The Architecture Content Framework ensures that all necessary aspects of the architecture are documented, making it easier to communicate the architecture to stakeholders and manage its development.

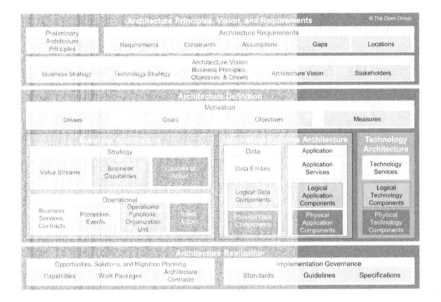

Figure 3: TOGAF Content Framework from the Open Group

TOGAF's Enterprise Continuum

The Enterprise Continuum is another important component of TOGAF. It is a classification system that helps organisations organise and understand the different elements of their architecture, from foundational models to specific solutions. The Enterprise Continuum is divided into two parts:

The Architecture Continuum: This includes more generic, reusable architecture elements, such as reference models and industry standards.

The Solutions Continuum: This includes more specific, implementation-focused elements, such as products and services tailored to the organisation's needs.

The Enterprise Continuum helps organisations manage the complexity of their architecture by organising it into manageable components and promoting the reuse of architectural assets.

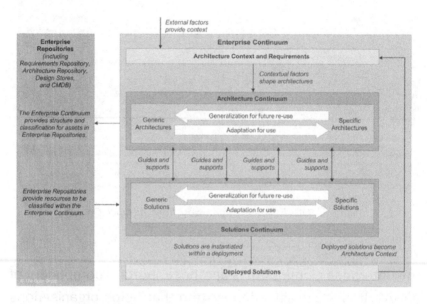

Figure 4: TOGAF Enterprise Continuum from the Open Group

Governance and Compliance

TOGAF places a strong emphasis on governance, ensuring that the architecture is managed effectively and remains aligned with business goals. This includes setting up governance structures, such as an Architecture Review Board, to oversee the development and implementation of the architecture. TOGAF also includes guidance on ensuring compliance with internal policies and external regulations, helping organisations manage risks and avoid costly mistakes.

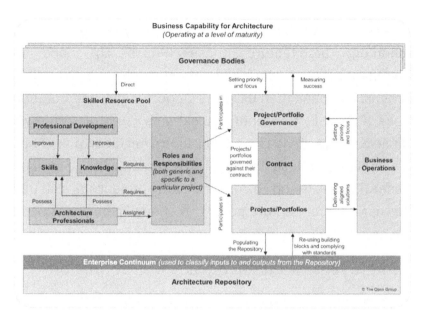

Figure 5: TOGAF Governance from the Open Group

Examples of TOGAF in Use

Example 1: Financial Institution Modernisation

A large financial institution uses TOGAF to guide its modernisation efforts. The bank is facing increasing pressure to improve its digital services, streamline operations, and ensure compliance with new regulations. By following the TOGAF ADM, the bank develops a comprehensive architecture vision that aligns with its strategic goals.

The business architecture phase (Phase B) focuses on optimising customer service processes, while the information systems architecture phase (Phase C) designs new data management systems to ensure regulatory compliance. The technology architecture phase (Phase D) plans the implementation of cloud infrastructure to support digital services. The bank then uses the Opportunities and Solutions phase (Phase E) to identify quick wins, such as improving mobile banking services, and develops a migration plan (Phase F) to implement these changes incrementally. The governance phases (Phases G and H) ensure that the project stays on track and that the architecture adapts to changing business needs over time.

Example 2: Government Agency Transformation

A government agency responsible for social services uses TOGAF to manage a large-scale transformation project. The agency needs to replace its outdated IT systems, which are hindering its ability to deliver services efficiently.

In the Preliminary Phase, the agency establishes an architecture board to oversee the project. The Architecture Vision phase (Phase A) focuses on improving service delivery through better data sharing and process automation. In the subsequent phases (B, C, D), the agency designs new business processes, data management systems, and a technology platform that supports inter-agency collaboration. The Migration Planning phase (Phase F) prioritises the replacement of critical systems and the phased rollout of new capabilities. TOGAF's governance framework ensures that the project complies with government standards and that stakeholders are engaged throughout the process.

Strengths of TOGAF

TOGAF has several strengths that contribute to its widespread adoption and effectiveness:

Comprehensive and Structured Approach

TOGAF provides a detailed, structured approach to developing and managing enterprise architecture. The ADM guides architects through each step of the process, ensuring that all necessary aspects are addressed. This comprehensive approach helps organisations manage complexity, align IT with business goals, and ensure that their architecture is well-documented and well-governed.

Flexibility and Adaptability

While TOGAF provides a structured methodology, it is also highly flexible and can be adapted to meet the specific needs of different organisations. The ADM is designed to be iterative, allowing organisations to tailor the process to their unique context and requirements. This flexibility makes TOGAF suitable for a wide range of industries and organisational sizes.

Focus on Governance and Compliance

TOGAF places a strong emphasis on governance, ensuring that the architecture is managed effectively and that it remains aligned with business objectives. The framework provides guidance on setting up governance structures, managing risks, and ensuring compliance with internal and external standards. This focus on governance helps organisations avoid costly mistakes and ensures that their architecture delivers value over the long term.

Encourages Reuse of Architectural Assets

TOGAF promotes the reuse of architectural assets through the Enterprise Continuum. By organising architecture into reusable components, TOGAF helps organisations avoid duplication of effort, reduce costs, and improve consistency across different projects and initiatives.

Widely Recognised and Supported

TOGAF is one of the most widely recognised and used EA frameworks globally. It has a large community of practitioners, extensive documentation, and a wealth of training and certification programs. This widespread recognition and support make it easier for organisations to adopt and implement TOGAF effectively.

Limitations of TOGAF

Despite its strengths, TOGAF has some limitations that organisations should be aware of:

Complexity and Steep Learning Curve

TOGAF's comprehensive nature, while a strength, also makes it complex and challenging to implement. The framework includes a vast amount of material, and mastering it requires significant time and effort. For organisations that are new to enterprise architecture, the learning curve can be steep, and there is a risk of becoming overwhelmed by the framework's complexity.

Potential for Over-Documentation

TOGAF's detailed approach can lead to an emphasis on producing extensive documentation. While thorough documentation is valuable, there is a risk of over-documentation, where the focus on creating artefacts overshadows the practical implementation and use of the architecture. This can lead to delays, increased costs, and reduced agility.

Lack of Prescriptive Tools and Techniques

While TOGAF provides a structured approach, it does not prescribe specific tools, techniques, or technologies for implementation. This can be a limitation for organisations that need more concrete guidance on how to execute the architecture. As a result, organisations must often supplement TOGAF with other methodologies, tools, or frameworks to meet their specific needs. Although many tools on the market claim to be, there are only a few certified tools and only till version 9.1 or 9.2.

TOGAF® Tool Certification Register

TOGAF 9 Certified Tools

There 7 tools from 7 organizations.

All tools listed below are certified for conformance to the TOGAF® Version 9.1 Specification or TOGAF® Version 9.2 Specification where advised.

Organization	Tool Name	First Certified	Renewal	Conformance Statement	Version
Avolution	ABACUS 6.0 or later	23-May-2012	23-May-2026		9.2
Bizzdesign	Bizzdesign Enterprise Studio	18-Jul-2012	18-Jul-2026		9.2
BOC Group	ADOIT	15-Sep-2017	15-Sep-2025		9.1
MEGA International	HOPEX Enterprise Architecture Suite	26-May-2015	26-May-2025		9.1
Orbus Software	iServer Business and IT Transformation Suite 2015 or later	19-Aug-2013	19-Aug-2025		9.2
Software AG	Alfabet	22-Jun-2012	22-Jun-2026		9.2
Software AG	ARIS 9.0 or later	19-Nov-2013	19-Nov-2025		9.1

Figure 6: List of TOGAF certificated tools from Open Group Website

Not Easily Aligned with Agile Practices

TOGAF's traditional approach, which involves extensive upfront planning and documentation, may not align well with Agile practices that prioritise flexibility, iteration, and minimal documentation. Organisations that are deeply invested in Agile methodologies may find it challenging to integrate TOGAF into their processes without significant customisation.

Focus on Large Enterprises

TOGAF is particularly well-suited for large organisations with complex IT environments. Smaller organisations with less complexity may find TOGAF's comprehensive approach to be overkill, leading to unnecessary complexity and effort. For these organisations, a more lightweight framework or a tailored version of TOGAF might be more appropriate.

TOGAF is a powerful and versatile framework that provides a comprehensive approach to developing and managing enterprise architecture. Its structured methodology, flexibility, and focus on governance make it a valuable tool for organisations looking to align their IT strategy with business goals, manage complexity, and drive transformation. However, its complexity, potential for over-documentation, and challenges in aligning with Agile practices are important considerations that organisations must manage carefully. By understanding both the strengths and limitations of TOGAF, organisations can effectively leverage the framework to achieve their strategic objectives while avoiding common pitfalls.

Federal Enterprise Architecture Framework (FEAF)

The Federal Enterprise Architecture Framework (FEAF) was developed by the U.S. federal government to guide the development and implementation of enterprise architecture within federal agencies. The need for such a framework arose in the 1990s as federal agencies were facing increasing pressure to modernise their IT systems, improve efficiency, and enhance inter-agency collaboration. The government recognised that a standardised approach to enterprise architecture could help address these challenges by providing a common framework for managing IT resources and aligning them with agency missions and goals.

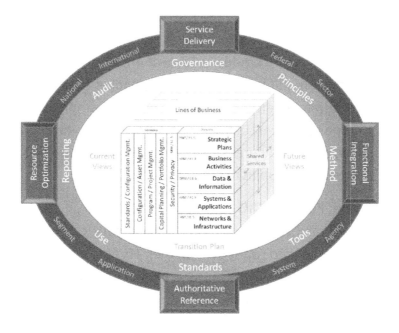

Figure 7: FRAF Model

History of FEAF

The development of FEAF was driven by several key legislative and executive actions:

1. **The Clinger-Cohen Act of 1996**: This legislation required federal agencies to implement IT management practices that aligned with their strategic goals and supported their missions. It also established the role of Chief Information Officers (CIOs) within federal agencies to oversee IT management and ensure compliance with the Act's requirements.

2. **The Office of Management and Budget (OMB) Circular A-130**: This circular provided policy guidance for the management of federal information resources, including the requirement for agencies to develop and maintain an enterprise architecture. It emphasised the importance of using architecture to ensure that IT investments were aligned with agency missions and provided value to taxpayers.

3. **The Federal CIO Council**: Established in 1996, the Federal CIO Council was tasked with promoting the efficient and effective use of IT across the federal government. The Council played a key role in the development of FEAF by providing guidance and support to agencies in their architecture efforts.

FEAF was first introduced in 1999 as a structured approach for developing enterprise architecture within federal agencies. It provided a set of guidelines, models, and tools that agencies could use to align their IT resources with their missions, improve efficiency, and enhance collaboration across agencies. Over time, FEAF has been updated and refined to reflect changes in technology, policy, and the evolving needs of the federal government.

How FEAF is Used for Enterprise Architecture

FEAF is designed to provide a standardised approach to enterprise architecture within federal agencies. It helps agencies develop and implement architectures that are aligned with their missions, support their strategic goals, and enable collaboration with other agencies.

The adoption of FEAF within federal agencies involves a systematic approach that ensures alignment with the agency's mission, strategic goals, and regulatory requirements. The process of adopting FEAF can be complex, as it requires careful planning, stakeholder engagement, and a commitment to continuous improvement. Here's how FEAF is typically adopted in a federal agency:

Establishing a Governance Structure

Initial Step: The first step in adopting FEAF is to establish a governance structure that will oversee the enterprise architecture efforts. This often involves creating an Architecture Review Board (ARB) or a similar body composed of senior leaders, IT professionals, and other key stakeholders. The ARB is responsible for setting the direction of the Enterprise Architecture initiative, making key decisions, and ensuring that the architecture aligns with the agency's strategic goals.

Ongoing Role: This governance structure plays a critical role throughout the adoption process, providing oversight, resolving issues, and ensuring that the Enterprise Architecture effort remains on track and compliant with federal regulations and standards.

Defining the Scope and Objectives

Assessment: The next step is to define the scope of the enterprise architecture effort and establish clear objectives. This involves assessing the current state of the agency's IT infrastructure, identifying key business processes, and understanding the strategic goals that the architecture needs to support.

Goal Setting: Agencies typically define specific objectives for their Enterprise Architecture efforts, such as improving interoperability, reducing IT costs, enhancing data sharing across departments, or supporting new technology initiatives. These objectives guide the development of the architecture and help ensure that it delivers value to the agency.

Engaging Stakeholders

Stakeholder Involvement: Successful adoption of FEAF requires the involvement of a broad range of stakeholders, including business units, IT departments, and external partners. Early engagement with stakeholders is crucial to ensure that their needs and concerns are addressed in the architecture.

Communication: Regular communication and collaboration with stakeholders help build support for the EA initiative, foster a shared understanding of the goals, and ensure that the architecture meets the needs of all parts of the organisation.

Developing the Architecture

Using the FEAF Framework: With the scope and objectives defined, the agency begins the process of developing its enterprise architecture using the FEAF framework. This involves creating detailed models and diagrams that represent the agency's business processes, data flows, applications, and technology infrastructure.

Iterative Process: The development of the architecture is typically an iterative process, with the framework being applied in phases. Agencies might start with a high-level architecture and then refine it over time, focusing on specific areas as needed. This phased approach allows for flexibility and ensures that the architecture can evolve in response to changing needs and priorities.

Implementing the Architecture

Integration with Existing Systems: Once the architecture is developed, the agency begins the process of implementing it. This often involves integrating new systems with existing IT infrastructure, migrating data, and possibly phasing out legacy systems that are no longer aligned with the agency's goals.

Change Management: Implementation also requires careful change management to ensure a smooth transition. Agencies must manage the impact on business processes, provide training for staff, and address any challenges that arise during the transition.

Continuous Improvement and Evolution

Monitoring and Evaluation: Adoption of FEAF is not a one-time effort but an ongoing process of improvement and evolution. Agencies need to continuously monitor the performance of their enterprise architecture, evaluate its effectiveness, and make adjustments as necessary.

Feedback Loops: Regular feedback from stakeholders and lessons learned from implementation are critical for refining the architecture. This ensures that it remains relevant and continues to provide value in a dynamic environment.

Ensuring Compliance and Reporting

Compliance with Federal Standards: Throughout the adoption process, agencies must ensure that their enterprise architecture complies with federal standards, policies, and regulations. FEAF provides guidance on how to meet these requirements, but it's the agency's responsibility to integrate compliance into their EA processes.

Reporting and Documentation: Agencies are often required to report on their Enterprise Architecture activities to oversight bodies such as the Office of Management and Budget (OMB). Comprehensive documentation of the architecture, its development, and its implementation is essential for meeting these reporting requirements.

Leveraging Best Practices and Lessons Learned

Benchmarking and Collaboration: Agencies adopting FEAF can benefit from leveraging best practices and lessons learned from other federal agencies. Collaboration and sharing of knowledge across agencies can help avoid common pitfalls and accelerate the adoption process.

Continuous Learning: As FEAF evolves and new versions are released, agencies need to stay informed about updates and adjust their EA practices accordingly. Continuous learning and adaptation are key to maintaining an effective and current enterprise architecture.

Examples of FEAF in Use

Example 1: Department of Homeland Security (DHS)

The Department of Homeland Security (DHS) uses FEAF to guide the development of its enterprise architecture. Given the complexity of its mission, which involves coordinating efforts across multiple agencies and jurisdictions, DHS relies on FEAF to ensure that its IT resources are aligned with its strategic goals and that they support effective collaboration with other federal, state, and local agencies. FEAF helps DHS standardise its IT infrastructure, improve interoperability, and enhance the efficiency of its operations.

Example 2: Environmental Protection Agency (EPA)

The Environmental Protection Agency (EPA) uses FEAF to manage its IT resources and ensure that they are aligned with the agency's mission to protect human health and the environment. By using FEAF, the EPA has been able to standardise its data management practices, improve information sharing with other agencies, and enhance the efficiency of its regulatory and enforcement activities. FEAF has also helped the EPA reduce costs by identifying opportunities for shared services and IT consolidation.

Example 3: Department of Defence (DoD)

The Department of Defence (DoD) employs FEAF to manage its complex IT infrastructure and ensure that it supports the agency's national security mission. FEAF helps the DoD align its IT investments with its strategic objectives, improve interoperability with other defence and intelligence agencies, and enhance the efficiency of its operations. FEAF also supports the DoD's efforts to modernise its IT infrastructure, reduce costs, and improve cybersecurity.

Strengths of FEAF

FEAF has several strengths that contribute to its effectiveness as a framework for enterprise architecture within federal agencies:

Standardisation and Interoperability

One of the key strengths of FEAF is its ability to promote standardisation and interoperability across federal agencies. By providing a common framework and set of standards, FEAF helps agencies develop architectures that are consistent with those of other agencies, enabling better collaboration and information sharing. This is particularly important in areas where multiple agencies need to work together, such as national security, public health, and disaster response.

Alignment with Strategic Goals

FEAF is designed to ensure that IT investments are aligned with an agency's strategic goals and missions. By using the framework, agencies can develop architectures that clearly link their IT resources to their mission-critical activities, ensuring that technology investments provide value and support the agency's objectives. This alignment is critical for ensuring that federal IT resources are used effectively and efficiently.

Focus on Efficiency and Cost-Effectiveness

FEAF encourages agencies to use their IT resources more efficiently and cost-effectively. By providing guidance on how to develop architectures that eliminate redundancies, optimise resource use, and streamline processes, FEAF helps agencies reduce costs and improve the efficiency of their operations. This is achieved through the identification of shared services, the consolidation of IT infrastructure, and the implementation of best practices.

Comprehensive Governance and Compliance Framework

FEAF provides a comprehensive framework for governance and compliance within federal agencies. It includes guidance on how to establish governance structures, such as Architecture Review Boards, to oversee the development and implementation of enterprise architecture. FEAF also helps agencies ensure compliance with federal policies, standards, and regulations, such as the Clinger-Cohen Act and OMB Circular A-130.

Scalability and Flexibility

FEAF is designed to be scalable and flexible, allowing it to be applied across a wide range of federal agencies with varying missions, sizes, and levels of complexity. The framework can be tailored to meet the specific needs of individual agencies, making it a versatile tool for managing enterprise architecture in the federal government.

Limitations of FEAF

Despite its strengths, FEAF has some limitations that agencies must consider when using the framework:

Complexity and Resource Requirements

FEAF can be complex and resource-intensive to implement, particularly for agencies that are new to enterprise architecture or that have limited resources. The framework requires a significant amount of time and effort to develop, implement, and maintain, which can be a barrier for some agencies. Smaller agencies or those with limited IT budgets may struggle to allocate the necessary resources to fully implement FEAF.

Potential for Over-Documentation

FEAF's emphasis on documentation can lead to a tendency for over-documentation, where the focus on creating artifacts overshadows the practical implementation and use of the architecture. This can result in excessive documentation that is time-consuming to produce and maintain, without necessarily providing proportional value. Over-documentation can also create challenges in keeping the architecture up to date, as changes in one area might require updates across multiple artifacts.

Difficulty in Adapting to Agile and Modern Practices

FEAF's traditional approach to enterprise architecture, which involves extensive upfront planning and documentation, may not align well with modern practices such as Agile development and DevOps, which prioritise flexibility, iteration, and rapid delivery. Agencies that have adopted or are moving towards these practices may find it challenging to integrate FEAF into their processes without significant customisation.

Limited Focus on Emerging Technologies

While FEAF provides a solid foundation for enterprise architecture, it may not fully address the challenges and opportunities presented by emerging technologies, such as cloud computing, artificial intelligence, and the Internet of Things (IoT). Agencies that are looking to adopt these technologies may need to supplement FEAF with additional frameworks, methodologies, or tools to effectively manage their integration into the architecture.

Risk of Siloed Implementation

Despite FEAF's goal of promoting standardisation and interoperability, there is a risk that agencies may implement the framework in a siloed manner, focusing solely on their internal architecture without considering the broader federal enterprise. This can lead to inconsistencies and challenges in achieving the desired level of collaboration and information sharing across agencies.

The Federal Enterprise Architecture Framework (FEAF) is a powerful and versatile tool for managing enterprise architecture within federal agencies. Its strengths lie in its ability to promote standardisation, align IT resources with strategic goals, and improve efficiency and cost-effectiveness. However, its complexity, potential for over-documentation, and challenges in adapting to modern practices are important considerations that agencies must manage carefully. By understanding both the strengths and limitations of FEAF, federal agencies can effectively leverage the framework to achieve their strategic objectives while avoiding common pitfalls.

Gartner's Enterprise Architecture Framework

History of Gartner's Enterprise Architecture Framework

Gartner, Inc., a leading research and advisory company, developed its Enterprise Architecture framework in response to the evolving needs of organisations to align their business strategies with their IT systems. Gartner's framework has its roots in the late 1990s and early 2000s, a period marked by rapid technological advancements and increasing complexity in IT environments. Organisations were struggling to manage their IT resources effectively while ensuring they supported business objectives. Gartner recognised the need for a more holistic approach to enterprise architecture that went beyond the traditional focus on IT infrastructure and emphasised the strategic alignment between business and IT.

Gartner's Enterprise Architecture framework emerged as a response to this need, offering a pragmatic and business-focused approach to enterprise architecture. Unlike other frameworks that are heavily prescriptive or technically oriented, Gartner's framework is known for its flexibility and emphasis on delivering business value. It is designed to **help organisations** navigate the complexities of modern IT environments, drive digital transformation, and ensure that their IT investments are closely aligned with their strategic goals.

Over the years, Gartner's framework has evolved to incorporate new trends and technologies, such as cloud computing, digital business models, and data-driven decision-making. It has become one of the most widely adopted and respected Enterprise Architecture frameworks in the industry, used by organisations around the world to guide their enterprise architecture practices.

Gartner

Figure 8: Gartner's Enterprise Architecture Delivery Framework

How Gartner's Enterprise Architecture Framework is Used

Gartner's Enterprise Architecture Framework is used as a strategic tool to help organisations align their IT systems with their business goals. It provides a flexible and adaptive approach to enterprise architecture that can be tailored to the unique needs of each organisation. The framework is typically used in the following ways:

Strategic Alignment of Business and IT

Goal Setting and Prioritisation: Gartner's EA framework emphasises the importance of aligning IT systems and initiatives with the organisation's strategic goals. It helps organisations identify the key business drivers and priorities, ensuring that IT investments and projects are directly linked to these strategic objectives.

Business Outcome-Driven Approach: The framework encourages a focus on business outcomes rather than just technical specifications. This means that enterprise architects are guided to start with the desired business results and work backward to design the IT systems that will support these outcomes.

Enabling Digital Transformation

Navigating Technological Change: Gartner's Enterprise Architecture framework is particularly well-suited for guiding organisations through digital transformation initiatives. It helps organisations assess the impact of emerging technologies, such as cloud computing, artificial intelligence, and the Internet of Things (IoT), and integrate them into their existing IT landscape in a way that supports business innovation.

Agility and Flexibility: The framework supports an agile approach to enterprise architecture, allowing organisations to adapt quickly to changing market conditions and technological advancements. This agility is crucial for organisations that need to stay competitive in a rapidly evolving digital landscape.

Managing Complexity in IT Environments

Simplifying Complex Architectures: Gartner's framework helps organisations manage the complexity of their IT environments by providing tools and methodologies for simplifying and rationalising IT systems. This includes identifying redundancies, optimising resource use, and ensuring that IT systems are scalable and adaptable.

Holistic View of the Enterprise: The framework encourages a holistic view of the enterprise, considering not just technology but also people, processes, and information. This comprehensive approach helps organisations ensure that all aspects of the enterprise are aligned and working together to achieve strategic goals.

Governance and Decision-Making

Establishing Governance Structures: Gartner's Enterprise Architecture framework provides guidance on establishing governance structures to oversee enterprise architecture initiatives. This includes setting up governance bodies, such as Architecture Review Boards, to ensure that architectural decisions are aligned with business goals and are made transparently and collaboratively.

Supporting Informed Decision-Making: The framework provides tools and methodologies for gathering and analysing data, enabling informed decision-making. This helps organisations make better choices about IT investments, technology adoption, and architectural changes.

Examples of Gartner's Framework in Use

Gartner's Enterprise Architecture Framework has been adopted by numerous organisations across various industries to align their IT strategies with business objectives, drive digital transformation, and manage complex IT environments. While specific details of firms using Gartner's Enterprise Architecture framework are often confidential due to the proprietary nature of enterprise architecture work, some generalised examples can provide insight into how different firms have implemented the framework.

Example 1: A Global Financial Institution

A large, multinational financial institution with operations in over 50 countries was facing significant challenges in managing its complex IT landscape. The bank had grown rapidly through acquisitions, leading to a fragmented IT environment with multiple redundant systems, disparate data sources, and inconsistent processes. The institution needed to modernise its IT infrastructure to remain competitive, improve customer experience, and comply with increasingly stringent regulatory requirements. Using Gartner's Enterprise Architecture framework, the bank went about to do the following:

Business Outcome Focus: The bank adopted Gartner's framework with a strong focus on aligning its IT architecture with strategic business outcomes. The framework helped the bank prioritise its IT initiatives based on key business objectives, such as enhancing customer experience, improving operational efficiency, and ensuring regulatory compliance.

Baseline Assessment and Gap Analysis: The bank began by conducting a comprehensive baseline assessment of its current IT environment, identifying redundancies, inefficiencies, and areas where systems were not aligned with business needs. This was followed by a gap analysis to determine where the bank's IT systems fell short of supporting its strategic goals.

Digital Transformation Strategy: The bank used Gartner's framework to guide its digital transformation strategy. This included the adoption of cloud computing to improve scalability and flexibility, the implementation of advanced data analytics to enhance decision-making, and the integration of new digital channels (e.g., mobile banking) to improve customer engagement. The framework provided a roadmap for implementing these technologies in a way that was aligned with the bank's business objectives.

Agile and Iterative Development: Recognising the need for agility, the bank adopted an iterative approach to enterprise architecture development. This allowed them to quickly implement changes, test new technologies, and make adjustments based on feedback and evolving business needs. The flexibility of Gartner's framework was crucial in enabling this agile approach.

Governance and Compliance: The bank established an Architecture Review Board to oversee the implementation of the enterprise architecture, ensuring that all decisions were aligned with business goals and regulatory requirements. Gartner's framework provided the governance structures needed to maintain accountability, transparency, and compliance throughout the transformation process.

The adoption of Gartner's Enterprise Architecture framework helped the bank streamline its IT environment, reducing redundancies and improving operational efficiency. The digital transformation initiatives led to a significant improvement in customer satisfaction, with enhanced digital services and faster, more reliable transaction processing. The bank achieved better regulatory compliance through standardised processes and improved data management capabilities. Overall, the framework enabled the bank to align its IT strategy with its long-term business objectives, driving growth and maintaining competitiveness in a rapidly evolving financial services industry.

Example 2: Large Manufacturing Company

A leading global manufacturer with a complex supply chain and production network was struggling to manage its sprawling IT systems. The company's rapid expansion into new markets and the acquisition of smaller firms had resulted in a disjointed IT landscape, with multiple ERP systems, legacy applications, and siloed data sources. The company needed to standardise its IT environment, improve visibility across its operations, and support its move towards smart manufacturing and Industry 4.0.

The manufacturing company adopted Gartner's Enterprise Architecture framework to ensure that its IT systems were aligned with its strategic goal of becoming a leader in smart manufacturing. The framework helped the company prioritise IT investments that would support automation, real-time data analytics, and integrated supply chain management.

Baseline Assessment: The Enterprise Architecture team conducted a thorough baseline assessment of the company's existing IT systems, identifying key areas of redundancy, inefficiency, and misalignment with business goals. This assessment provided a clear understanding of the current state and informed the development of the future-state architecture.

Simplification and Standardisation: Using Gartner's framework, the company developed a roadmap for simplifying and standardising its IT environment. This involved consolidating multiple ERP systems into a single, unified platform, phasing out legacy applications, and implementing standardised data management practices. The framework's tools for managing complexity were instrumental in guiding these efforts.

Integration with Industry 4.0 Technologies: The company leveraged Gartner's framework to integrate emerging Industry 4.0 technologies, such as IoT sensors, robotics, and AI-driven analytics, into its manufacturing processes. The framework helped ensure that these technologies were implemented in a way that supported the company's broader strategic objectives, such as improving production efficiency, reducing downtime, and enhancing supply chain visibility.

Governance and Agility: The company established a governance framework based on Gartner's recommendations, including the creation of an Architecture Review Board to oversee the Enterprise Architecture initiative. The agile, iterative approach encouraged by Gartner's framework allowed the company to quickly adapt to new opportunities and challenges, ensuring that the architecture remained aligned with its evolving business needs.

The company successfully standardised its IT environment, leading to significant cost savings, improved operational efficiency, and better visibility across its global operations. The integration of Industry 4.0 technologies enhanced the company's manufacturing capabilities, enabling more flexible and responsive production processes. The governance structures established under Gartner's framework ensured that the architecture remained aligned with the company's strategic goals, supporting ongoing innovation and growth.

Strengths of Gartner's Enterprise Architecture Framework

Gartner's Enterprise Architecture Framework offers several strengths that make it a valuable tool for organisations looking to align their IT systems with business goals and drive digital transformation:

Business Outcome-Focused

Strategic Alignment: One of the key strengths of Gartner's framework is its focus on business outcomes. The framework encourages organisations to start with their desired business results and design their IT systems and architecture to support these outcomes. This ensures that IT investments are closely aligned with business goals and deliver tangible value to the organisation.

Flexibility and Adaptability

Customisable Approach: Gartner's Enterprise Architecture framework is highly flexible and can be tailored to meet the unique needs of each organisation. Unlike more rigid frameworks, it allows organisations to adapt the approach to their specific business context, industry, and technological landscape. This flexibility is particularly valuable in dynamic environments where business needs and technologies are constantly evolving.

Support for Digital Transformation

Guiding Innovation: The framework is well-suited for guiding organisations through digital transformation initiatives. It provides tools and methodologies for assessing the impact of emerging technologies and integrating them into the existing IT landscape. This support for innovation helps organisations stay competitive in a rapidly changing digital environment.

Comprehensive and Holistic View

Integrated Approach: Gartner's Enterprise Architecture framework takes a holistic view of the enterprise, considering not just technology but also people, processes, and information. This comprehensive approach ensures that all aspects of the enterprise are aligned and working together to achieve strategic goals. It also helps organisations manage complexity and avoid the silos that can develop in more narrowly focused frameworks.

Emphasis on Agility

Enabling Agility: The framework supports an agile approach to enterprise architecture, allowing organisations to adapt quickly to changing market conditions and technological advancements. This agility is crucial for organisations that need to respond rapidly to new opportunities and challenges.

Limitations of Gartner's Enterprise Architecture Framework

While Gartner's Enterprise Architecture Framework offers many strengths, it also has some limitations that organisations should be aware of:

Requires Strong Leadership and Support

Dependence on Executive Buy-In: The successful adoption of Gartner's Enterprise Architecture framework requires strong leadership and support from the organisation's executives. Without this top-down commitment, the Enterprise Architecture initiative may struggle to gain the necessary resources, attention, and priority. Organisations with weak or inconsistent leadership may find it challenging to fully realise the benefits of the framework.

Resource-Intensive

Demanding Process: Implementing Gartner's Enterprise Architecture framework can be resource-intensive, requiring significant time, effort, and expertise. Organisations need to invest in building a dedicated Enterprise Architecture team, conducting thorough assessments, and developing detailed architecture models. Smaller organisations or those with limited resources may find it challenging to allocate the necessary resources to fully implement the framework.

Complexity in Large Organisations

Managing Complexity: While the framework is designed to help manage complexity, its comprehensive and holistic approach can also add to the complexity, particularly in large organisations with diverse business units and IT environments. Managing the framework across such a large and varied enterprise can be challenging, requiring careful coordination and communication.

Potential for Over-Analysis

Risk of Analysis Paralysis: The emphasis on thorough analysis and strategic alignment can sometimes lead to over-analysis or "analysis paralysis", where the organisation becomes bogged down in the planning and design phases. This can delay implementation and result in missed opportunities. Organisations need to strike a balance between analysis and action to avoid this pitfall.

Integration with Agile Methodologies

Challenges with Agile Integration: While the framework supports agility, integrating it with Agile development methodologies can be challenging. The structured nature of enterprise architecture may sometimes conflict with the iterative and fast-paced nature of Agile development. Organisations need to carefully manage this integration to ensure that the benefits of both approaches are realised.

Gartner's Enterprise Architecture Framework is distinct from other frameworks due to its strong focus on aligning IT architecture with business outcomes, offering a business-centric rather than a purely technical approach. Unlike more prescriptive frameworks like TOGAF or FEAF, Gartner's framework is highly flexible and adaptable, allowing organisations to tailor it to their specific needs and environments. This flexibility, combined with an emphasis on agility, makes Gartner's framework particularly effective for navigating digital transformation and managing complex, rapidly changing IT environments. Additionally, Gartner's approach integrates a holistic view of the enterprise, considering people, processes, and technology, and emphasises strong but adaptable governance structures. Another key differentiator is the access to Gartner's ongoing research and industry insights, which provides organisations with up-to-date best practices and strategic guidance. This makes Gartner's framework a powerful tool for organisations seeking to align their IT systems with business goals, drive innovation, and manage complexity in a dynamic business landscape.

Ministry of Defence Architecture Framework (MoDAF)

The Ministry of Defence Architecture Framework (MoDAF) is a specialised enterprise architecture framework developed by the United Kingdom's Ministry of Defence (MoD) to support the design and management of defence systems. MoDAF was created in response to the growing complexity of defence operations and the need for a standardised approach to managing the various systems, processes, and information flows within the MoD. This was a very similar programme to FEAF where it was driven by the public sector but in this case, it was specifically for the military just like the U.S. Department of Defence Architecture Framework (DoDAF).

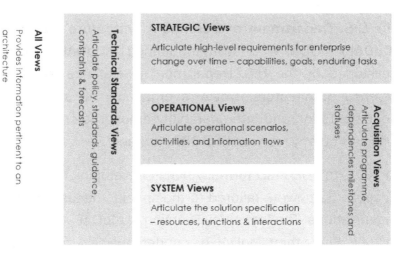

Figure 9: High level view of MoDAF

History of MoDAF

MoDAF has its roots in the late 1990s and early 2000s, a period when the UK Ministry of Defence recognised the need for a comprehensive architecture framework to manage its increasingly complex defence systems. The development of MoDAF was influenced by several earlier architecture frameworks, including:

TOGAF (The Open Group Architecture Framework): TOGAF provided foundational concepts for enterprise architecture, influencing the structure and methodology of MODAF.

The Zachman Framework: The Zachman Framework's focus on providing a structured way of viewing and organising enterprise architecture influenced MODAF's approach to handling different perspectives within the defence domain.

The U.S. Department of Defence Architecture Framework (DoDAF): MODAF was heavily influenced by DoDAF, which was developed by the U.S. Department of Defence to manage defence architecture. DoDAF's emphasis on standardised documentation and interoperability among defence systems was particularly relevant to MODAF's objectives.

In 2001, the UK MoD formally began developing MODAF as a bespoke framework tailored to the specific needs of defence organisations. The first official version of MoDAF was released in 2005. Since then, MoDAF has undergone several updates to incorporate new technologies, methodologies, and best practices. It remains a key tool used by the UK Ministry of Defence and other defence organisations to manage the architecture of their systems and operations.

How MoDAF is Used by Organisations

MODAF is primarily used within the defence sector, particularly by the UK Ministry of Defence and allied defence organisations. It provides a structured approach to designing, managing, and communicating the architecture of defence systems, ensuring that these systems are aligned with strategic objectives, interoperable, and capable of supporting complex defence operations. The framework is used in several key ways:

Design and Development of Defence Systems

System Architecture Design: MoDAF is used to guide the design and development of defence systems, including weapons systems, command and control systems, and communication networks. The framework provides a set of viewpoints and models that help architects and engineers understand the system's structure, behaviour, and interactions with other systems. These models ensure that the system is designed to meet the operational requirements and is aligned with the overall defence strategy.

Interoperability: One of the critical uses of MoDAF is to ensure interoperability among different defence systems. Given the complex and integrated nature of modern defence operations, it is essential that different systems can work together seamlessly. MODAF provides tools and methodologies for ensuring that systems are designed with interoperability in mind, using standardised data formats, communication protocols, and interfaces.

Strategic Planning and Decision-Making

Alignment with Defence Strategy: MoDAF is used to ensure that defence systems and operations are aligned with the overarching strategic objectives of the Ministry of Defence. The framework provides tools for mapping out how different systems support strategic goals, such as national security, force projection, and defence readiness. This alignment helps decision-makers understand how investments in technology and systems contribute to broader defence outcomes.

Scenario Planning and Risk Management: MoDAF supports strategic planning by providing tools for scenario planning and risk management. By modelling different scenarios and analysing potential risks, defence planners can make informed decisions about the development, deployment, and management of defence systems. This capability is particularly important in the defence sector, where the ability to respond to rapidly changing threats and environments is critical.

Communication and Collaboration

Common Language and Framework: MoDAF provides a common language and set of standards for communication and collaboration among different stakeholders within the defence sector. This includes military personnel, engineers, architects, procurement officers, and external contractors. The framework's standardised models and viewpoints ensure that everyone involved in the design and management of defence systems has a shared understanding of the architecture and can collaborate effectively.

Documentation and Reporting: MoDAF is also used to create detailed documentation and reports that describe the architecture of defence systems. These documents are essential for communicating the design and operation of systems to stakeholders, ensuring compliance with regulatory requirements, and supporting audits and reviews. The framework provides templates and guidelines for creating these documents, ensuring that they are consistent and comprehensive.

Lifecycle Management of Defence Systems

System Lifecycle Management: MoDAF is used to manage the entire lifecycle of defence systems, from initial concept and design through to deployment, operation, and eventual decommissioning. The framework provides tools for tracking the status of systems throughout their lifecycle, ensuring that they are maintained, upgraded, and replaced as needed. This lifecycle management is critical for ensuring that defence systems remain effective and capable of meeting evolving operational requirements.

Continuous Improvement: MoDAF supports continuous improvement by providing tools for analysing system performance, identifying areas for enhancement, and implementing changes. This iterative approach ensures that defence systems are continually refined and improved to meet new challenges and take advantage of emerging technologies.

Strengths of MoDAF

MODAF has several strengths that make it a valuable tool for managing the architecture of defence systems:

Tailored for Defence Needs

Defence-Specific Focus: MoDAF is specifically designed for the defence sector, making it highly relevant and effective for managing the unique challenges of defence operations. Unlike more general-purpose frameworks, MoDAF addresses the specific requirements of defence systems, such as interoperability, security, and alignment with military strategies.

Comprehensive and Structured Approach

Viewpoints and Models: MoDAF provides a comprehensive set of viewpoints and models that cover all aspects of defence architecture. This structured approach ensures that every aspect of the system, from technical design to strategic alignment, is considered and documented. The use of standardised models also facilitates communication and collaboration among stakeholders.

Ensures Interoperability

Standardisation: One of the key strengths of MoDAF is its focus on ensuring interoperability among defence systems. The framework provides tools for standardising data formats, interfaces, and communication protocols, ensuring that different systems can work together seamlessly. This interoperability is critical for the success of integrated defence operations, where different systems must coordinate and share information in real-time.

Facilitates Strategic Planning

Alignment with Strategic Objectives: MoDAF is designed to ensure that defence systems are aligned with the strategic objectives of the Ministry of Defence. The framework provides tools for mapping out how systems support strategic goals, enabling decision-makers to make informed choices about investments and deployments. This strategic alignment ensures that defence systems contribute effectively to broader defence outcomes.

Supports Lifecycle Management

Comprehensive Lifecycle Management: MoDAF supports the entire lifecycle of defence systems, from initial concept to decommissioning. This comprehensive approach ensures that systems are maintained, upgraded, and replaced as needed, ensuring that they remain effective and capable of meeting operational requirements throughout their lifecycle.

Limitations of MODAF

Despite its strengths, MODAF also has some limitations that organisations should be aware of:

Complexity

Steep Learning Curve: MoDAF is a complex framework that requires significant expertise to implement effectively. The comprehensive set of viewpoints, models, and methodologies can be overwhelming, particularly for organisations that are new to enterprise architecture or that have limited resources. The complexity of the framework can lead to challenges in adoption and implementation.

Resource Intensive

High Resource Requirements: Implementing MoDAF requires significant time, effort, and resources. The need for specialised training, detailed documentation, and continuous management can strain the resources of defence organisations, particularly smaller or less well-funded entities. The resource-intensive nature of MODAF can also make it difficult to implement in organisations with limited capacity.

Focus on Defence Sector

Limited Applicability Outside Defence: MoDAF is specifically designed for the defence sector, which means it may not be directly applicable to other industries or sectors. Organisations outside the defence sector may find that MoDAF's focus on military operations, interoperability, and security does not align with their needs. This limits the broader applicability of the framework.

Rigid Structure

Potential Lack of Flexibility: While MoDAF's structured approach is one of its strengths, it can also be a limitation. The rigid structure of the framework may make it difficult to adapt to the unique needs or circumstances of specific defence organisations. Organisations that require a more flexible or adaptive approach to enterprise architecture may find MoDAF too constraining.

Evolving Needs and Technology

Challenges in Keeping Up with Rapid Technological Change: The defence sector is characterised by rapid technological change, with new technologies emerging that can quickly render existing systems obsolete. While MoDAF is designed to manage the lifecycle of defence systems, it may struggle to keep pace with the rapid evolution of technology. Organisations may need to supplement MoDAF with additional frameworks or methodologies to ensure that their architecture remains current and capable of integrating emerging technologies.

MoDAF is a powerful and specialised enterprise architecture framework designed to meet the unique needs of the defence sector. Its strengths lie in its tailored focus on defence operations, comprehensive and structured approach, emphasis on interoperability, and support for strategic planning and lifecycle management. However, its complexity, resource-intensive nature, and limited applicability outside the defence sector are important considerations that organisations must manage carefully. By understanding both the strengths and limitations of MoDAF, defence organisations can effectively leverage the framework to design, manage, and improve their systems, ensuring that they are aligned with strategic objectives and capable of supporting complex defence operations.

Dragon1 Framework

The Dragon1 Framework is an enterprise architecture framework that emphasises visualisation, communication, and a business-driven approach to managing complex IT systems and aligning them with organisational goals. Dragon1 provides tools for creating clear, intuitive visual models of an organisation's architecture, making it accessible to both technical and non-technical stakeholders. This visual and flexible approach helps organisations bridge the gap between business and IT, drive transformation and innovation, and manage complexity effectively by simplifying the design, management, and communication of their enterprise architecture.

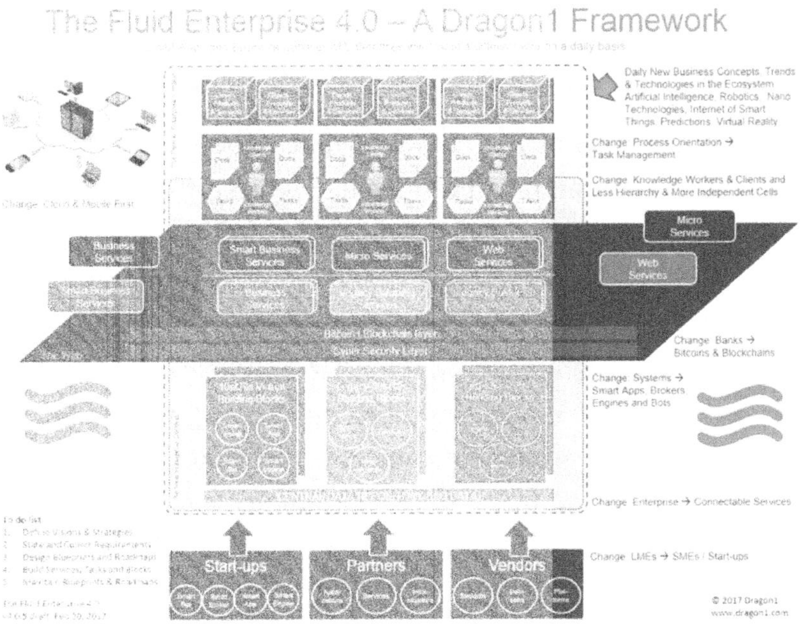

Figure 10: Dragon1 Framework for dynamic enterprises

History of the Dragon1 Framework

The Dragon1 Framework is a relatively **modern enterprise architecture (EA) framework that originated in the Netherlands.** It was developed by Mark Paauwe and his team in the early 2000s as a response to the growing complexity of enterprise systems and the need for a more visual, **business-driven** approach to enterprise architecture. Unlike **many traditional** Enterprise Architecture frameworks, Dragon1 places a strong emphasis on visualisation, communication, and practical

99

application, aiming to bridge the gap between business and IT through a more intuitive and accessible method.

Dragon1 was born out of the recognition that existing Enterprise Architecture frameworks were often too rigid, complex, and technically oriented to effectively engage business stakeholders. Mark Paauwe, a Dutch enterprise architect, recognised the need for a framework that not only provided a comprehensive approach to enterprise architecture but also made it easier for non-technical stakeholders to understand and participate in the architecture process. Paauwe and his team developed Dragon1 with the goal of making enterprise architecture more business-driven, visual, and practical.

The framework was initially introduced in the early 2000s and has since been adopted by a range of organisations, particularly in Europe. Dragon1 has evolved over time, incorporating feedback from practitioners and adapting to new technological trends and business needs. It has gained recognition for its innovative approach to enterprise architecture, particularly its focus on visual communication and the practical implementation of architecture within organisations.

How Dragon1 is Used

Dragon1 is used by organisations to design, manage, and communicate their enterprise architecture in a way that aligns with business strategy and drives transformation. The framework is particularly valued for its emphasis on visualisation, which makes it easier for organisations to understand and work with complex architectures. Dragon1 is used in several key ways:

Visualising Enterprise Architecture

Architecture Visualisations: One of the core components of Dragon1 is its focus on visualisations. Organisations use Dragon1 to create visual representations of their enterprise architecture, including business processes, data flows, application landscapes, and IT infrastructure. These visualisations are designed to be intuitive and easy to understand, making it easier for stakeholders from across the organisation to engage with the architecture and provide input.

Communication Tool: The visual nature of Dragon1 makes it an effective tool for communication. By creating clear, visual representations of the architecture, organisations can bridge the gap between business and IT, ensuring that all stakeholders have a shared understanding of the enterprise's systems and processes. This improved communication helps to align IT initiatives with business goals and fosters collaboration across different departments.

Aligning Business and IT

Business-Driven Approach: Dragon1 is designed to ensure that enterprise architecture is closely aligned with business strategy. Organisations use the framework to map out how their

IT systems and processes support business objectives, identify areas where improvements can be made, and prioritise initiatives that deliver the most value to the business. This business-driven approach helps to ensure that IT investments are aligned with the organisation's strategic goals.

Transformation and Innovation: The framework supports organisations in driving business transformation and innovation. By providing tools for visualising and analysing the current state of the architecture, Dragon1 helps organisations identify opportunities for improvement, plan transformation initiatives, and implement changes in a way that supports business growth and innovation.

Managing Complexity

Simplifying Complex Systems: Dragon1 is particularly useful for managing the complexity of modern enterprise systems. The framework provides tools for breaking down complex architectures into manageable components, creating visualisations that make it easier to understand and work with these systems. Organisations use Dragon1 to identify redundancies, optimise resource use, and ensure that their architecture is scalable and adaptable.

Scenario Planning and Decision-Making: Dragon1 supports scenario planning and decision-making by allowing organisations to create different models of their architecture and analyse the potential impact of changes. This helps organisations make informed decisions about how to evolve their architecture, manage risks, and respond to changing business needs.

Examples of Dragon1

Dragon1 has been successfully used by a variety of organisations across different industries. Here are some examples of how the framework has been applied:

Example 1: Financial Services Company

A large financial services company was struggling with a fragmented IT landscape, with multiple legacy systems, siloed data, and a lack of alignment between IT and business strategy. The company needed to modernise its IT infrastructure, improve data integration, and ensure that its IT systems supported its growth objectives.

The company adopted Dragon1 to create a visual representation of its enterprise architecture. By mapping out its current IT landscape and identifying areas of misalignment, the company was able to develop a clear roadmap for modernisation. The visualisations created using Dragon1 helped to communicate the architecture to both business and IT stakeholders, ensuring that everyone was on the same page and aligned with the company's strategic goals.

The company successfully implemented its modernisation strategy, consolidating its IT systems, improving data integration, and aligning IT with business objectives. The use of Dragon1 facilitated better communication and collaboration between business and IT, resulting in a more agile and responsive IT environment that supported the company's growth.

Example 2: Healthcare Organisation

A large healthcare organisation needed to improve its patient care processes by integrating its electronic health records (EHR) system with other healthcare applications and ensuring compliance with regulatory requirements. The organisation faced challenges in visualising the complex interactions between different systems and aligning IT initiatives with patient care objectives.

The healthcare organisation used Dragon1 to create visual models of its enterprise architecture, including the EHR system, patient care processes, and data flows. These visualisations made it easier for stakeholders to understand the architecture, identify areas for improvement, and ensure that IT initiatives were aligned with the organisation's patient care objectives.

The organisation successfully integrated its EHR system with other healthcare applications, improving the efficiency of patient care processes and ensuring compliance with regulatory requirements. The use of Dragon1's visualisations helped to facilitate communication between IT and healthcare professionals, resulting in a more coordinated and effective approach to patient care.

Strengths of the Dragon1 Framework

Dragon1 has several strengths that make it a valuable tool for organisations looking to manage and improve their enterprise architecture:

Emphasis on Visualisation

Intuitive and Accessible: One of the key strengths of Dragon1 is its emphasis on visualisation. The framework's focus on creating clear, visual representations of the architecture makes it easier for non-technical stakeholders to understand and engage with complex systems. This accessibility helps to bridge the gap between business and IT, ensuring that all stakeholders have a shared understanding of the architecture.

Business-Driven Approach

Alignment with Business Strategy: Dragon1 is designed to ensure that enterprise architecture is closely aligned with business strategy. The framework's business-driven approach helps organisations prioritise IT initiatives that deliver the most value to the business, ensuring that IT investments are aligned with strategic goals.

Flexibility and Adaptability

Customisable Framework: Dragon1 is highly flexible and can be adapted to meet the specific needs of different organisations. The framework can be customised to fit the organisation's industry, size, and complexity, making it suitable for a wide range of applications.

Support for Transformation and Innovation

Driving Change: Dragon1 supports organisations in driving transformation and innovation. The framework provides tools for identifying opportunities for improvement, planning transformation initiatives, and implementing changes in a way that supports business growth and innovation.

Limitations of the Dragon1 Framework

Despite Its strengths, Dragon1 also has some limitations that organisations should be aware of:

Learning Curve

Complexity in Implementation: While Dragon1's emphasis on visualisation makes it more accessible to non-technical stakeholders, the framework itself can be complex to implement. Organisations may need to invest in training and resources to fully leverage the framework's capabilities, particularly if they are new to enterprise architecture.

Resource Requirements

Investment in Tools and Training: Implementing Dragon1 effectively may require significant investment in tools, training, and resources. Organisations need to ensure that they have the necessary expertise and infrastructure to support the use of the framework.

Focus on Visualisation

Potential for Over-Reliance on Visuals: While visualisation is one of Dragon1's key strengths, there is a potential risk of over-reliance on visuals at the expense of detailed analysis and documentation. Organisations need to strike a balance between visual communication and the detailed, technical work required to implement and manage complex architectures.

The Dragon1 Framework is a powerful and innovative tool for managing enterprise architecture, particularly valued for its emphasis on visualisation and business-driven approach. It has been successfully used by organisations across various industries to align IT with business strategy, drive transformation, and manage complexity. However, organisations considering Dragon1 should be aware of its learning curve and resource requirements, and ensure that they are prepared to invest in the tools and training needed to fully leverage the framework's capabilities. By understanding both the strengths and limitations of Dragon1, organisations can effectively use the framework to achieve their strategic objectives and improve their enterprise architecture.

Organising an Enterprise Architecture Team

An effective Enterprise Architecture team is critical to the success of the enterprise architecture function within an organisation. The structure of an Enterprise Architecture team can vary depending on the organisation's size, complexity, and industry. Before we begin, lets revisit what IT architecture is.

IT Architecture: A Conceptual Overview

Conceptually, an IT architecture can be defined as:

- **The fundamental organisation of a system,**

- **Embodied in its components,**

- **Their relationships to each other and the environment,**

- **And the principles governing its design and evolution.**

This definition underscores the idea that IT architecture is not just about the technical components but about the relationships and interactions between these components and their environment. It's about understanding how the whole system works together to deliver value and achieve strategic objectives.

Practically, an IT architecture is represented through **Architectural Descriptions** from the viewpoints of various stakeholders. These descriptions are captured in a structured way to ensure that every perspective—whether from business leaders, IT managers, end-users, or external partners—is considered and aligned.

Different **Architecture Views** are created to address the concerns of different stakeholders:

- **Business View**: Focuses on how the architecture supports business processes and goals.

- **Data View**: Describes how data is structured, stored, and accessed.

- **Application View**: Details how applications interact and integrate within the system.

- **Technology View**: Provides a technical blueprint of the infrastructure and networks.

By using these views, architects ensure that the architecture is comprehensive, coherent, and aligned with both current and future needs. This, in turn, ensures that the system remains "alive" and relevant, much like the environments that Christopher Alexander describes.

With this in mind, we can start defining the type of roles we would need to build a more comprehensive Enterprise Architecture team to develop on each of these views and perspectives.

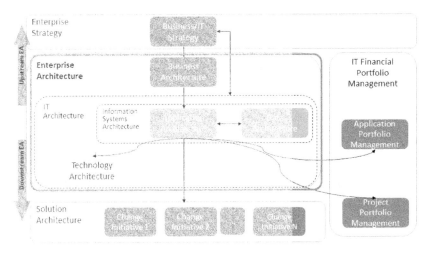

Figure 11: Relationship between the various architectures

111

Chief Architect

The leader of the Enterprise Architecture team holds a pivotal role within an organisation, responsible for shaping the strategic direction of its enterprise architecture. This role is not only about managing the architecture itself but also about ensuring that it aligns seamlessly with the organisation's strategic goals and vision. As the primary architect of the organisation's digital and technological landscape, this leader plays a crucial role in guiding the organisation through its digital transformation journey, optimising business processes, and driving innovation.

Setting the Strategic Direction for Enterprise Architecture

The leader of the Enterprise Architecture team is tasked with **setting the strategic direction** for the organisation's enterprise architecture. This involves defining a clear vision and roadmap for the Enterprise Architecture function, ensuring that it supports the overall business strategy and helps achieve the desired outcomes. The strategic direction encompasses a variety of aspects:

Aligning Technology with Business Goals

The Enterprise Architecture leader ensures that the architecture is not just a technical blueprint but a strategic asset that supports the organisation's mission, objectives, and business strategy. This involves aligning technology investments and initiatives with business priorities, such as enhancing customer experience, improving operational efficiency, or enabling new digital services.

Identifying Future Trends and Opportunities

Part of setting the strategic direction is to stay ahead of technological trends and understand how they could impact the organisation. The Enterprise Architecture leader must be forward-thinking, identifying opportunities for leveraging emerging technologies (like AI, machine learning, cloud computing, and IoT) to create competitive advantages.

Developing a Multi-Year Architectural Roadmap

The EA leader creates a roadmap that outlines the key architectural initiatives over a multi-year period. This roadmap is dynamic and evolves based on changing business needs, market conditions, and technological advancements. It provides a clear path for transitioning from the current state to the target architecture, detailing the milestones, priorities, and dependencies.

Overseeing the Development and Implementation of Architecture

The Enterprise Architecture leader is responsible for **overseeing the development** of the enterprise architecture and ensuring its successful implementation across the organisation. This involves several key activities:

Architectural Governance and Standards

The Enterprise Architecture leader establishes architectural governance frameworks, policies, and standards that guide the development and implementation of architecture within the organisation. This ensures consistency, compliance, and alignment across all IT projects and initiatives. For example, setting standards for API design, data security, and cloud architecture ensures that different teams are working within a unified framework.

Managing Cross-Functional Teams

Developing an enterprise architecture requires collaboration across various teams, including IT, business units, cybersecurity, and data management. The Enterprise Architecture leader acts as a bridge between these teams, fostering collaboration, resolving conflicts, and ensuring that architectural designs meet both technical requirements and business objectives.

Ensuring Flexibility and Scalability

The Enterprise Architecture leader ensures that the architecture is designed to be flexible and scalable, allowing the organisation to adapt to changing market conditions and business requirements. This involves selecting the right architecture patterns (such as microservices, serverless computing, or event-driven architecture) that can scale with the organisation's growth and evolving needs.

Risk Management and Mitigation

The Enterprise Architecture leader plays a critical role in identifying architectural risks, such as technology obsolescence, vendor lock-in, or cybersecurity threats, and developing strategies to mitigate these risks. This ensures that the architecture remains robust, secure, and future-proof.

Communicating the Architecture to Senior Leadership and Stakeholders

One of the most critical responsibilities of the Enterprise Architecture leader is to **communicate the architecture** to senior leadership and other stakeholders. Effective communication is essential for gaining buy-in, securing funding, and ensuring alignment across the organisation. This involves several aspects:

Articulating the Value of Architecture

The Enterprise Architecture leader must clearly communicate how the architecture supports the organisation's strategic goals and delivers business value. This involves presenting complex architectural concepts in a way that non-technical stakeholders can understand, highlighting the benefits, such as cost savings, improved agility, enhanced customer experience, and reduced risk.

Facilitating Stakeholder Engagement

The Enterprise Architecture leader engages with a wide range of stakeholders, from C-level executives to department heads and IT teams. They must build strong relationships with these stakeholders, listen to their needs and concerns, and ensure that the architecture addresses their priorities. Regular communication, workshops, and architectural reviews are essential for maintaining alignment and fostering a collaborative environment.

Providing Regular Updates and Reports

The Enterprise Architecture leader provides regular updates on the progress of architectural initiatives, the achievement of key milestones, and any changes to the architectural roadmap. This transparency helps build trust and ensures that stakeholders are aware of how the architecture is evolving to meet the organisation's needs.

Driving Architectural Decisions and Approvals

As the leader of the Enterprise Architecture team, this role is responsible for driving key architectural decisions and obtaining approvals from senior leadership. This requires a deep understanding of both the technical and business implications of architectural choices and the ability to present a compelling case for why certain decisions are being made.

The leader of the Enterprise Architecture team is a strategic visionary, a skilled communicator, and a catalyst for change. By setting the strategic direction for the organisation's enterprise architecture, overseeing its development and implementation, and effectively communicating with stakeholders, the EA leader ensures that the architecture becomes a powerful enabler of business success. This role requires a balance of technical expertise, strategic thinking, leadership, and communication skills to drive innovation, optimise operations, and align technology with business goals.

The next few roles are more functional and only be a high level description would be covered in this chapter. Each role would be explained in greater details in subsequent chapters.

Enterprise Architect

The Enterprise Architect is responsible for the overarching design and management of the entire enterprise architecture. This role involves coordinating the work of other architects and ensuring that all aspects of the architecture are aligned with the organisation's strategic objectives.

Key Responsibilities:

Architectural Integration: The Enterprise Architect ensures that all components of the architecture, including business processes, data, applications, technology, and security, are integrated and work together cohesively.

Architecture Development: This role involves developing and maintaining the enterprise architecture framework, methodologies, and standards, ensuring that they are aligned with the organisation's goals and best practices.

Strategic Alignment: The Enterprise Architect works closely with business and IT leaders to ensure that the architecture supports the organisation's strategic objectives and enables business transformation.

Governance and Oversight: This role involves establishing governance structures and processes to oversee the development and implementation of the architecture, ensuring compliance with standards and policies.

Business Architect

Focuses on aligning business processes with the overall business strategy. They work with business leaders to identify key processes and areas for improvement, ensuring that the IT infrastructure supports these processes. This role involves working closely with business units to understand their needs, processes, and goals, and translating these into architectural requirements.

Key Responsibilities:

Business Strategy Alignment: The Business Architect works with business leaders to ensure that the architecture aligns with the organisation's strategic goals and supports its business processes.

Process Modelling: This role involves mapping out the organisation's business processes, identifying inefficiencies, and working to optimise and standardise these processes across the enterprise.

Requirements Gathering: The Business Architect gathers and analyses business requirements, translating them into architectural designs that support the organisation's objectives.

Stakeholder Collaboration: This role requires close collaboration with business units, ensuring that their needs are represented in the architecture and that the architecture delivers value to the business.

Technology Architect

Responsible for the design and implementation of the IT infrastructure. This includes selecting the appropriate technologies, designing the network and systems architecture, and ensuring that the technology aligns with business needs. This role involves designing and managing the organisation's hardware, networks, and other IT infrastructure components.

Key Responsibilities:

Infrastructure Design: The Technology Architect designs the organisation's IT infrastructure, including servers, storage, networking, and cloud environments, ensuring that it supports the enterprise's applications and data needs.

Infrastructure Security: This role involves implementing security measures to protect the organisation's infrastructure from threats, ensuring compliance with security policies and regulatory requirements.

Scalability and Performance: The Technology Architect ensures that the infrastructure is scalable and performs optimally, supporting the organisation's growth and providing a reliable foundation for its applications and services.

Disaster Recovery and Continuity: This role involves designing and implementing disaster recovery and business continuity plans to ensure that the organisation can recover quickly from disruptions and continue operating.

Information Architect

Manages the organisation's data and information assets. They design data models, ensure data quality, and work to ensure that information flows efficiently across the organisation. This role focuses on ensuring that data is organised, accessible, and aligned with the organisation's business needs.

Key Responsibilities:

Data Modelling: The Information Architect creates and maintains data models that represent the organisation's data entities, relationships, and flows. These models ensure that data is structured in a way that supports business processes and decision-making.

Data Governance: This role involves establishing data governance policies and practices to ensure the accuracy, consistency, and security of the organisation's data.

Information Lifecycle Management: The Information Architect is responsible for managing the entire lifecycle of the organisation's data, from creation and storage to archiving and disposal.

Data Integration: This role involves ensuring that data from different sources is integrated effectively, enabling seamless data sharing and reporting across the organisation.

Security Architect

Ensures that the organisation's IT systems are secure. They design and implement security measures to protect data, systems, and networks from threats, and work closely with other architects to ensure that security is integrated into all aspects of the architecture.

Key Responsibilities:

- **Security Strategy**: The Security Architect develops and implements a security strategy that aligns with the organisation's business objectives and regulatory requirements.

- **Risk Assessment and Management**: This role involves conducting risk assessments to identify potential security threats and vulnerabilities, and implementing measures to mitigate these risks.

- **Security Controls Implementation**: The Security Architect designs and implements security controls, such as firewalls, encryption, access controls, and intrusion detection systems, to protect the organisation's assets.

- **Compliance and Audit**: This role involves ensuring that the organisation's security architecture complies with relevant laws, regulations, and standards, and supporting audits and assessments as needed.

Integration Architect

Focuses on ensuring that different systems and applications within the organisation can work together seamlessly. They design and implement integration strategies, ensuring that data and processes can flow between systems without issues. This role focuses on ensuring that different IT systems, whether on-premises or cloud-based, work together seamlessly to support business processes and deliver a unified user experience.

Key Responsibilities:

Integration Strategy Development: The Integration Architect develops and implements the organisation's integration strategy, ensuring that it aligns with the overall enterprise architecture and business goals. This includes selecting the appropriate integration platforms, tools, and methodologies to connect disparate systems.

System Interoperability: This role involves designing and overseeing the implementation of integration solutions that ensure interoperability between different systems and applications. The Integration Architect ensures that data and processes can flow smoothly between systems, eliminating silos and enhancing operational efficiency.

Middleware and API Management: The Integration Architect manages middleware technologies and Application Programming Interfaces (APIs) that facilitate communication between systems. This includes designing and implementing

APIs, ensuring they are secure, scalable, and meet the organisation's integration requirements.

Data Integration and Synchronisation: This role includes designing and implementing data integration solutions that ensure data consistency and synchronisation across systems. The Integration Architect works to prevent data duplication, reduce errors, and ensure that accurate and up-to-date information is available across the enterprise.

Integration Governance: The Integration Architect establishes governance processes to manage and oversee integration activities, ensuring that they comply with the organisation's standards, security policies, and best practices. This includes setting up guidelines for API usage, data sharing, and system connectivity.

Troubleshooting and Optimisation: This role involves monitoring integration solutions to identify and resolve issues, optimise performance, and ensure the reliability of system integrations. The Integration Architect continuously looks for ways to improve integration processes and enhance system interoperability.

Collaboration with Stakeholders: The Integration Architect works closely with business units, IT teams, and external vendors to understand integration needs, develop solutions, and ensure that integration efforts are aligned with business objectives. This collaboration is key to delivering integration solutions that meet the needs of all stakeholders.

Solutions Architect

Works on specific projects, designing and implementing solutions that meet the business requirements. They collaborate with other architects to ensure that the solutions align with the overall enterprise architecture. This role bridges the gap between the high-level enterprise architecture and the detailed design of individual systems or projects.

Key Responsibilities:

Solution Design: The Solution Architect designs comprehensive solutions that meet specific business requirements, integrating various components, such as applications, data, and infrastructure.

Project Leadership: This role involves leading the design and implementation of projects, ensuring that solutions are delivered on time, within budget, and meet quality standards.

Technical Expertise: The Solution Architect provides technical expertise and guidance to project teams, ensuring that solutions are technically sound and aligned with the broader enterprise architecture.

Stakeholder Communication: This role requires close communication with business stakeholders, project managers, and technical teams to ensure that solutions meet business needs and are implemented successfully.

Application Architect

The Application Architect is responsible for designing the organisation's application landscape, ensuring that applications are aligned with business needs and are integrated effectively across the enterprise.

Key Responsibilities:

Application Design and Development: The Application Architect designs the architecture for enterprise applications, ensuring that they meet business requirements and are scalable, reliable, and maintainable.

Application Integration: This role involves designing and implementing integration solutions that enable different applications to work together seamlessly, supporting end-to-end business processes.

Technology Selection: The Application Architect evaluates and selects the appropriate technologies, frameworks, and tools for developing and deploying applications within the organisation.

Application Lifecycle Management: This role involves managing the entire lifecycle of enterprise applications, from initial design and development to deployment, maintenance, and eventual retirement.

Each role in an Enterprise Architecture team is critical to the success of the organisation's architecture efforts. From strategic leadership provided by the Chief Enterprise Architect to the technical expertise of the Application and Technology Architects, each team member contributes to ensuring that the enterprise architecture aligns with business goals, supports innovation, and manages complexity effectively. By working together, the Enterprise Architecture team can create a cohesive and robust architecture that drives the organisation's success.

Architecture Competencies

Here is a table that summarises the competencies matrix for an architect.

	What you KNOW	What you DO	What you ARE
Technology	• In-depth understanding of the domain and pertinent technologies • Understand what technical issues are key to success • Development methods and modelling techniques	• Modelling • Tradeoff analysis • Prototype/experiment/simulate • Prepare architectural documents and presentations • Technology trend analysis/roadmaps • Take a system viewpoint	• Creative • Investigative • Practical/pragmatic • Insightful • Tolerant of ambiguity, willing to backtrack, seek multiple solutions • Good at working at an abstract level
Consulting	• Elicitation techniques • Consulting frameworks	• Build 'trusted advisor' relationships • Understand what the developers want and need from the architecture • Help developers see the value of the architecture and understand how to use it successfully • Mentor junior architects	• Committed to others' success • Empathetic, approachable • An effective change agent, process savvy • A good mentor, teacher
Strategy	• Your organisation's business strategy and rationale • Your competition (products, strategies and processes) • Your company's business practices	• Influence business strategy • Translate business strategy into technical vision and strategy • Understand customer and market trends • Capture customer, organisational and business requirements on the architecture	• Visionary • Entrepreneurial
Organisational Politics	• Who the key players are in the organisation • What they want, both business and personal	• Communicate, communicate, communicate! • Listen, network, influence • Sell the vision, keep the vision alive • Take and retake the pulse of all critical influencers of the architecture project	• Able to see from and sell to multiple viewpoints • Confident and articulate • Ambitious and driven • Patient and not • Resilient • Sensitive to where the power is and how it flows in your organisation
Leadership	• Yourself	• Set team context (vision) • Make decisions (stick) • Build teams • Motivate	• You and others see you as a leader • Charismatic and credible • You believe it can and should be done, and that you can lead the effort • You are committed, dedicated, passionate • You see the entire effort in a broader business and personal context

The Enterprise Architect

The role of the Enterprise Architect is crucial in ensuring that an organisation's IT infrastructure aligns with its business goals. As covered earlier, the Enterprise Architect is responsible for designing, overseeing, and evolving the enterprise architecture to meet the organisation's strategic objectives. This chapter delves into the skills necessary for an Enterprise Architect, how they perform their job, best practices for success, and suggested learning exercises to develop and hone these skills.

Skills Necessary for an Enterprise Architect

To be effective in their role, an Enterprise Architect must possess a diverse set of skills that span both technical and business domains. These skills enable the Enterprise Architect to design comprehensive and scalable architectures, align IT with business strategy, and communicate effectively with various stakeholders.

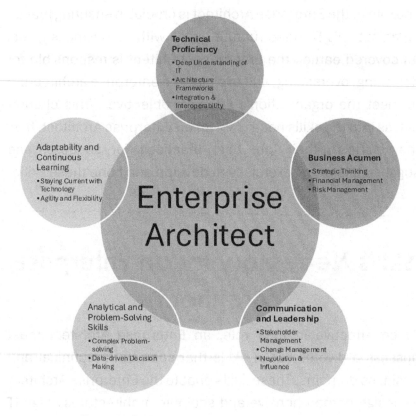

Figure 12: Skills necessary for an Enterprise Architect

Technical Proficiency

Technical proficiency is a cornerstone of the Enterprise Architect's role, requiring a deep understanding of various IT systems, including software, hardware, networks, and databases. This expertise extends to knowledge of cloud computing, data management, cybersecurity, and emerging technologies, all of which are critical for designing robust and future-proof architectures. A good Enterprise Architect should have familiarity with architecture frameworks such as TOGAF, Zachman, and working knowledge of design languages such as ArchiMate is also essential. The ability to adopt and implement these frameworks can provide a more structured approach to developing and managing enterprise architecture effectively.

Additionally, the Enterprise Architect must be skilled in designing systems that integrate seamlessly with one another, ensuring smooth data flow and interoperability across the organisation. This ability to create cohesive, well-integrated systems is vital for supporting the organisation's overall strategic goals and operational efficiency.

Business Acumen

Business acumen is another critical skill set for an Enterprise Architect, as it enables them to understand and navigate the organisation's business model, goals, and challenges effectively. This includes strategic thinking, where the Enterprise Architect must align IT initiatives with the broader business strategy and anticipate how emerging technologies can drive business growth and innovation. In addition to strategic alignment, the Enterprise Architect must possess strong financial management skills, including knowledge of budgeting, cost management, and financial analysis. These skills are essential for justifying IT investments and demonstrating their value to the organisation, ensuring that resources are allocated efficiently and effectively. Furthermore, the Enterprise Architect must be proficient in risk management, with the ability to identify and mitigate risks associated with IT projects. This includes understanding and addressing technological, operational, and strategic risks that could impact the success of the enterprise architecture and the organisation.

Communication and Leadership

Effective communication and leadership are crucial for an Enterprise Architect to successfully engage with a diverse range of stakeholders, including executives, business leaders, IT teams, and external partners. The Enterprise Architect must be adept at stakeholder management, ensuring that the needs and concerns of all parties are understood and addressed throughout the architectural process. Leading organisational change is another key responsibility of the Enterprise Architect. This involves guiding the organisation through technological and process transitions, ensuring smooth adoption with minimal disruption to operations. Additionally, the Enterprise Architect must possess strong negotiation and influence skills. This is essential for advocating for architectural decisions that align with the organisation's long-term goals, even when these decisions may require significant upfront investments or shifts in direction. The ability to communicate the value and rationale behind these decisions is critical to securing the necessary buy-in and support from stakeholders.

Analytical and Problem-Solving Skills

The Enterprise Architect must excel in analytical and problem-solving skills to navigate the complexities of enterprise architecture. This includes the ability to analyse complex problems, identify their root causes, and develop innovative, practical, and scalable solutions. Whether dealing with integration challenges, legacy system constraints, or evolving business requirements, the Enterprise Architect needs to approach problems with a structured and strategic mindset. Furthermore, data-driven decision-making is an essential skill for an Enterprise Architect. Leveraging data and analytics allows the Enterprise Architect to make informed architectural decisions, justify those decisions with evidence, and measure their outcomes effectively. This approach ensures that architectural strategies are not only theoretically sound but also grounded in real-world data and aligned with business objectives.

Adaptability and Continuous Learning

In the rapidly evolving technology landscape, an Enterprise Architect must prioritise adaptability and continuous learning to remain effective in their role. Staying current with the latest trends, tools, and methodologies is crucial for designing architectures that are not only relevant today but also "future-proof". Continuous learning enables the Enterprise Architect to incorporate new technologies and best practices into the architecture, keeping the organisation at the forefront of innovation. Additionally, the Enterprise Architect must demonstrate agility and flexibility, being able to quickly adapt to changes in the business environment and respond to new challenges and opportunities as they arise. This ability to pivot and adjust strategies ensures that the enterprise architecture remains aligned with the organisation's goals, even in the face of uncertainty or disruption.

How an Enterprise Architect Performs Their Job

The Enterprise Architect's role is dynamic and multifaceted, involving both strategic planning and hands-on implementation. They play a crucial role in ensuring that an organisation's IT systems are aligned with its strategic goals and are capable of supporting current and future business needs. Below is a detailed look at how an Enterprise Architect typically performs their job, from assessing the current state to advocating for the architecture's value within the organisation.

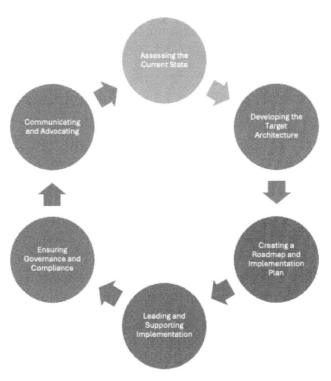

Figure 13: Typical Enterprise Architect's job flow

Assessing the Current State

The first step in the Enterprise Architect's process is conducting a thorough enterprise analysis. This involves assessing the current state of the organisation's IT systems, processes, and overall architecture. The Enterprise Architect maps out the existing technology landscape, identifying both strengths and weaknesses. This assessment provides a clear understanding of how well the current architecture supports the organisation's business goals and where improvements are needed. In addition to this technical analysis, the EA engages in stakeholder interviews across the organisation. These interviews are crucial for gaining a comprehensive understanding of business needs, identifying pain points, and clarifying the organisation's strategic objectives. By combining technical analysis with stakeholder input, the Enterprise Architect builds a solid foundation for developing a future-oriented architecture.

Developing the Target Architecture

Once the current state has been assessed, the Enterprise Architect moves on to developing a vision and strategy for the target architecture. This vision is carefully aligned with the organisation's strategic goals, ensuring that the architecture supports long-term business objectives. The Enterprise Architect sets out long-term goals for IT systems, identifies key initiatives, and defines the desired future state of the enterprise architecture. With this vision in place, the Enterprise Architect then creates detailed architectural designs that outline how the organisation's IT systems will evolve to meet future needs. This phase includes designing new systems, modifying existing ones, and ensuring that all components of the architecture are well-integrated and interoperable. The architectural design serves as a blueprint for the organisation's IT transformation.

Creating a Roadmap and Implementation Plan

After defining the target architecture, the Enterprise Architect develops a comprehensive roadmap that outlines the steps required to transition from the current state to the desired future state. This roadmap includes defining milestones, prioritising initiatives based on their strategic importance, and setting realistic timelines for implementation. With the roadmap in hand, the Enterprise Architect collaborates closely with project managers, IT teams, and business units to develop detailed implementation plans. These plans involve allocating resources, setting budgets, and establishing governance structures to oversee the execution of the roadmap. The implementation plan ensures that the transition to the new architecture is well-coordinated, efficient, and aligned with the organisation's goals.

Leading and Supporting Implementation

During the implementation phase, the Enterprise Architect takes on a leadership role, providing oversight and guidance to ensure that projects are executed according to the architectural design. The Enterprise Architect ensures that the implementation stays on track with the roadmap, addressing any deviations or challenges that arise. Problem-solving is a key aspect of this role; as projects progress, the Enterprise Architect must be prepared to address any issues that emerge, making necessary adjustments to the architecture or implementation plans. This hands-on involvement ensures that the architecture remains adaptable and responsive to any unforeseen challenges, maintaining alignment with the organisation's strategic objectives.

Ensuring Governance and Compliance

A critical responsibility of the Enterprise Architect is establishing governance structures to oversee the development, implementation, and ongoing management of the enterprise architecture. This includes setting up an Architecture Review Board, defining standards and policies, and ensuring that all architectural decisions comply with regulatory requirements. Governance ensures that the architecture is developed in a controlled and consistent manner, with appropriate oversight and accountability. The Enterprise Architect also engages in continuous monitoring and improvement of the architecture. By gathering feedback and data, the Enterprise Architect identifies areas for improvement, ensuring that the architecture remains aligned with business goals and is adaptable to the organisation's evolving needs.

Communicating and Advocating

Effective communication is essential for the success of enterprise architecture initiatives. The Enterprise Architect regularly communicates with stakeholders to keep them informed about the progress of architectural projects, gather feedback, and address any concerns. Maintaining open lines of communication is key to ensuring stakeholder buy-in and support throughout the architectural process. Additionally, the Enterprise Architect plays an advocacy role within the organisation, championing the value of enterprise architecture. By demonstrating how the architecture contributes to achieving strategic objectives and driving **business success,** the Enterprise Architect ensures that enterprise architecture is recognised as a critical enabler of organisational growth and innovation.

Best Practices for Success as an Enterprise Architect

To be successful as an Enterprise Architect, **certain best** practices should be followed:

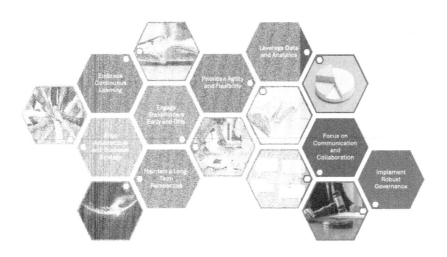

Figure 14: Enterprise Architecture Best Practices

Align Architecture with Business Strategy

It is crucial that the enterprise architecture is consistently aligned with the organisation's strategic goals. This alignment ensures that IT investments are purposeful and contribute directly to the organisation's long-term objectives. By aligning the architecture with the business strategy, the Enterprise Architect can clearly demonstrate the value of IT initiatives, showing how they support the overarching goals of the organisation. This strategic alignment also ensures that the architecture is not just a technical blueprint but a critical enabler of business success.

Engage Stakeholders Early and Often

Building strong relationships with stakeholders from the beginning is essential for successful enterprise architecture. Engaging stakeholders early in the architectural process allows the Enterprise Architect to understand their needs, gather valuable input, and ensure that the architecture reflects these insights. Regular communication with stakeholders throughout the process is key to building trust, ensuring alignment with business goals, and securing the necessary support for architectural initiatives. This ongoing engagement helps prevent misunderstandings and ensures that the architecture is well-supported across the organisation.

Embrace Continuous Learning

In a rapidly evolving technology landscape, continuous learning is vital for the success of an Enterprise Architect.

Staying current with the latest trends, tools, and methodologies in both technology and business ensures that the architect can effectively adapt to new challenges and leverage emerging opportunities. Committing to ongoing education allows the Enterprise Architect to incorporate the latest innovations into the architecture, ensuring that it remains relevant and effective in meeting the organisation's needs.

Prioritise Agility and Flexibility

Designing architectures that are flexible and adaptable to change is essential in today's dynamic business environment. The ability to pivot and respond quickly to new business requirements, technological advancements, or market changes ensures that the enterprise architecture remains relevant and effective. An agile architecture allows the organisation to stay competitive and responsive to opportunities, ensuring that IT systems can support evolving business strategies without being a barrier to innovation.

Leverage Data and Analytics

Using data and analytics to inform architectural decisions is a best practice that ensures the architecture is based on evidence rather than assumptions. Data-driven decision-making allows the Enterprise Architect to measure the impact of initiatives accurately and make adjustments as needed. By leveraging analytics, the architect can demonstrate the effectiveness of the architecture in achieving business goals, providing a clear rationale for decisions and ensuring that IT investments are delivering the expected value.

Focus on Communication and Collaboration

Strong communication and collaboration skills are fundamental to the success of an Enterprise Architect. Creating an environment of open communication, where ideas can be shared freely and feedback is encouraged, is essential for fostering collaboration between business and IT teams. This collaborative approach ensures that all stakeholders are working towards common goals, reducing the risk of misalignment and ensuring that the architecture supports the organisation's objectives. Effective communication also helps to build consensus and secure buy-in for architectural initiatives.

Maintain a Long-Term Perspective

While addressing immediate needs is important, it is equally essential for an Enterprise Architect to maintain a long-term perspective. Designing architectures that are scalable and sustainable ensures that they can support the organisation's growth and evolution over time. By keeping the long-term vision in mind, the architect can create systems that not only meet current demands but also remain relevant and effective as the organisation changes and grows.

Implement Robust Governance

Establishing strong governance structures is critical for overseeing the development and implementation of enterprise architecture. Effective governance ensures that architectural decisions are made transparently, align with established standards, and are consistent with the organisation's strategic objectives. Governance structures such as an Architecture Review Board help to maintain accountability, enforce standards, and provide a framework for making informed decisions that support the long-term success of the enterprise architecture.

Learning Exercises to Develop Enterprise Architecture Skills

To develop and refine the skills necessary for success as an Enterprise Architect, consider the following learning exercises:

Case Study Analysis

Engaging in case study analysis is a valuable exercise for developing critical thinking and problem-solving skills, particularly in the field of enterprise architecture. By analysing both successful and unsuccessful enterprise architecture initiatives, you can identify the key factors that contributed to their outcomes, such as strategic alignment, stakeholder engagement, and risk management. Reflecting on how you would approach similar challenges in your own organisation allows you to apply these lessons practically. This exercise not only sharpens your analytical abilities but also provides insights into the complexities and nuances of enterprise architecture, helping you to develop more effective strategies in your own work.

Simulation Exercises

Participating in simulation exercises offers a practical way to apply theoretical knowledge in a controlled, risk-free environment. In these simulations, you are tasked with designing and implementing an enterprise architecture for a hypothetical organisation. This hands-on experience allows you to experiment with different approaches, make decisions, and see the immediate impact of those decisions on the overall architecture. Through these exercises, you can improve your decision-making and strategic planning skills, as well as gain confidence in your ability to manage complex architectural projects in real-world settings.

Framework Mastery

Mastering popular architecture frameworks such as TOGAF, Zachman, or Dragon1 is essential for any Enterprise Architect. These frameworks provide structured methodologies, tools, and best practices that are widely recognised and used across the industry. By taking a deep dive into these frameworks, studying their principles, and practicing applying them to real-world scenarios, you can enhance your ability to design and manage enterprise architectures effectively. Understanding the strengths and limitations of each framework allows you to choose the right approach for your organisation's needs and ensures that your architectural strategies are grounded in proven methodologies.

Cross-Functional Collaboration

Engaging in cross-functional projects is an excellent way to improve your communication and stakeholder management skills. By collaborating with different business units, IT teams, and external partners, you gain a broader perspective on the organisation's needs and challenges. This collaboration helps you to understand the diverse viewpoints and priorities within the organisation, allowing you to design architectures that are more aligned with business objectives. Additionally, working across functions enhances your ability to build consensus, manage conflicts, and ensure that all stakeholders are committed to the success of the architectural initiatives.

The Business Architect

The role of the Business Architect is crucial in ensuring that an organisation's business strategy is effectively translated into actionable and sustainable processes, systems, and structures. The Business Architect serves as a bridge between the strategic goals of the business and the technical execution carried out by IT teams. This chapter will explore the skills necessary for a Business Architect, how they perform their job, best practices for success, and some suggested learning exercises to help develop and refine these skills.

Skills Necessary for a Business Architect

To excel as a Business Architect, a combination of strategic, analytical, and interpersonal skills is essential. The following are key skills required for the role:

Figure 15: Skills Necessary for a Business Architect

Strategic Thinking

A deep understanding of the organisation's business model, industry trends, and competitive landscape is critical for a Business Architect. This business acumen enables the Business Architect to identify opportunities for improvement and innovation that align with the organisation's strategic goals. By understanding the broader context in which the organisation operates, the Business Architect can ensure that the business processes and systems support the long-term objectives of the organisation. Additionally, the ability to develop a clear vision of the desired future state and create a roadmap to achieve that vision is essential. This involves setting long-term goals and identifying the necessary steps to align business processes with strategic objectives, ensuring that the organisation remains competitive and agile in a rapidly changing market.

Analytical and Problem-Solving Skills

Proficiency in process modelling techniques, such as Business Process Model and Notation (BPMN), is crucial for a Business Architect. This skill allows the Business Architect to map out existing business processes, identify inefficiencies, and design optimised processes that improve performance. By visualising how different processes interact and flow within the organisation, the Business Architect can pinpoint areas for enhancement and streamline operations to better support the organisation's goals. Additionally, the ability to analyse data to inform business decisions is essential. The Business Architect should be comfortable working with data to identify trends, measure performance, and justify changes to business processes. This analytical approach ensures that decisions are based on evidence and that any changes made are grounded in a solid understanding of their potential impact.

Communication and Collaboration

Effective stakeholder management is a key responsibility for a Business Architect. The ability to engage with a wide range of stakeholders, including executives, business leaders, and IT teams, is essential for gathering input, building consensus, and ensuring that everyone is aligned with the business strategy. Strong communication skills are necessary to articulate complex ideas clearly and to foster an environment where stakeholders feel heard and involved. In addition to communication, the ability to facilitate workshops, lead discussions, and negotiate solutions that satisfy the needs of various stakeholders is crucial. The Business Architect must be adept at mediating conflicts and finding common ground to move initiatives forward, ensuring that the business architecture reflects a balanced and inclusive approach.

Change Management

The Business Architect plays a vital role in leading organisational change, guiding the organisation through transitions in a way that minimises disruption and maximises adoption. This leadership in transformation involves managing resistance, communicating the benefits of change, and ensuring that new processes and systems are adopted smoothly and effectively. Additionally, identifying and mitigating risks associated with business transformation is a critical skill for the Business Architect. By anticipating potential challenges and developing strategies to address them proactively, the Business Architect helps to ensure that changes are implemented successfully, and that the organisation can navigate the complexities of transformation with confidence.

Technical Knowledge

While the role of a Business Architect is not as technically focused as other roles within enterprise architecture, a solid understanding of the organisation's IT systems is essential. This technical knowledge allows the Business Architect to align business needs with IT capabilities, ensuring that the technology infrastructure supports and enhances business processes. Understanding how different systems interact and support the organisation's goals is crucial for designing business architectures that are both effective and sustainable. Additionally, familiarity with enterprise architecture frameworks, such as TOGAF or Zachman, is beneficial. These frameworks provide structured approaches to aligning business processes with IT architecture, helping the Business Architect to create cohesive and integrated solutions that drive the organisation's success.

How a Business Architect Performs Their Job

The Business Architect's role is multifaceted, involving strategic planning, process modelling, stakeholder engagement, and change management. Here's how a Business Architect typically performs their job:

Understanding the Business Strategy

The first step for a Business Architect is to gain a deep understanding of the organisation's business strategy, goals, and objectives. This involves engaging with executives and business leaders to understand their vision for the future and the challenges they face. The Business Architect uses this information to identify areas where business processes need to be aligned or improved to support the organisation's strategic direction.

Analysing and Modelling Business Processes:

The Business Architect conducts a thorough analysis of the organisation's current business processes. This involves mapping out existing processes, identifying inefficiencies, and analysing how these processes align with the organisation's strategic goals. The Business Architect uses process modelling techniques to visualise these processes, making it easier to identify areas for improvement and design optimised processes that better support the business strategy.

Developing Business Architecture

Based on the analysis, the Business Architect develops a comprehensive business architecture that aligns with the organisation's strategic objectives. This architecture includes a detailed description of the business processes, organisational structures, and information flows that support the business strategy. The Business Architect also identifies the necessary changes to existing processes and systems to achieve the desired future state.

Engaging Stakeholders

Throughout the process, the Business Architect engages with stakeholders across the organisation to gather input, build consensus, and ensure alignment with the business strategy. This involves facilitating workshops, leading discussions, and negotiating solutions that meet the needs of various stakeholders. Effective stakeholder management is critical for ensuring that the business architecture is well-supported and that changes are implemented successfully.

Leading Change Management

The Business Architect plays a key role in leading organisational change. This includes developing change management strategies, managing resistance, and ensuring that changes are adopted smoothly and effectively. The Business Architect works closely with change management teams to communicate the benefits of the changes, provide training and support, and monitor the adoption of new processes and systems.

Monitoring and Continuous Improvement

After implementing changes, the Business Architect monitors the performance of the new processes and systems to ensure that they are delivering the expected benefits. This involves collecting data, analysing performance metrics, and identifying areas for further improvement. The Business

Architect continuously refines the business architecture to ensure that it remains aligned with the organisation's strategic goals and is capable of adapting to changing business needs.

Best Practices for Success as a Business Architect

To be successful as a Business Architect, certain best practices should be followed:

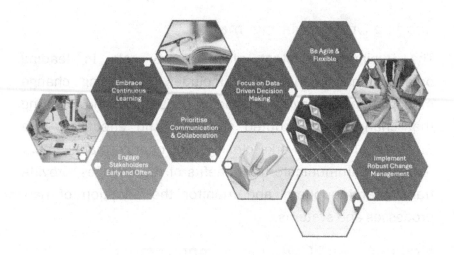

Figure 16: Best Practices for Success as a Business Architect

Align Business Architecture with Strategic Goals

It is essential to ensure that the business architecture is always closely aligned with the organisation's strategic goals. This alignment is crucial because it demonstrates the value of business process improvements and ensures that the architecture supports the organisation's long-term objectives. By aligning the architecture with the broader strategic direction of the organisation, the Business Architect helps to create systems and processes that not only meet immediate needs but also contribute to sustained success and competitive advantage over time.

Engage Stakeholders Early and Often

Building strong relationships with stakeholders from the beginning of any business architecture initiative is vital. Engaging stakeholders early in the process allows the Business Architect to understand their needs, gather valuable input, and build consensus around the proposed solutions. Regular communication with stakeholders throughout the process is key to building trust, ensuring alignment with business goals, and securing the necessary support for successful implementation. This proactive engagement helps to prevent misunderstandings and ensures that the architecture is well-supported across the organisation.

Prioritise Communication and Collaboration

Strong communication and collaboration skills are fundamental to the success of a Business Architect. It is important to foster an environment where open communication is encouraged, allowing ideas to be shared freely and feedback to be actively sought and considered. Collaborating with business units, IT teams, and external partners ensures that everyone involved is working towards common goals. This collaborative approach not only helps in aligning different perspectives but also strengthens the overall effectiveness of the business architecture.

Embrace Continuous Learning

In a constantly evolving business environment, successful Business Architects are those who commit to continuous learning. Staying current with the latest trends, tools, and methodologies in both business and technology is essential for adapting to new challenges and leveraging emerging opportunities. Continuous learning enables the Business Architect to incorporate innovative solutions and best practices into the architecture, ensuring that it remains relevant and capable of supporting the organisation's evolving needs.

Focus on Data-Driven Decision Making

Using data and analytics to inform decisions is a best practice that ensures business architecture is based on evidence rather than assumptions. Data-driven decision-making allows the Business Architect to measure the impact of initiatives accurately and make adjustments as needed. By relying on data, the architect can provide a clear rationale for decisions, demonstrate the effectiveness of the architecture, and ensure that business processes are optimised for performance and efficiency.

Be Agile and Flexible

Designing business architectures that are flexible and adaptable to change is essential in today's dynamic business landscape. The ability to pivot and respond quickly to new business requirements, market changes, or technological advancements ensures that the business architecture remains relevant and effective. An agile architecture allows the organisation to stay competitive and responsive to opportunities, ensuring that business processes can support evolving strategies without being a barrier to innovation.

Implement Robust Change Management

Developing and implementing strong change management strategies is critical to ensuring that business process changes are adopted smoothly and effectively. Effective change management minimises resistance, ensures stakeholder buy-in, and helps achieve the desired outcomes. By carefully planning and managing the transition, the Business Architect can ensure that new processes and systems are integrated seamlessly into the organisation, leading to sustained improvements and the successful realisation of business goals.

Learning Exercises to Develop Business Architecture Skills

To develop and refine the skills necessary for success as a Business Architect, consider the following learning exercises:

Case Study Analysis

Analyse case studies of successful and unsuccessful business architecture initiatives. Identify the key factors that contributed to their outcomes, and reflect on how you would approach similar challenges. This exercise will help you develop critical thinking and problem-solving skills.

Process Modelling Workshops

Participate in or lead process modelling workshops where you map out existing business processes and design optimised processes that align with strategic goals. These workshops provide hands-on experience with process modelling techniques and improve your ability to analyse and design business processes.

Cross-Functional Projects

Engage in cross-functional projects where you collaborate with different business units, IT teams, and external partners. This exercise will help you improve your communication, collaboration, and stakeholder management skills.

Framework Mastery

Take a deep dive into popular business architecture frameworks and methodologies, such as TOGAF, BPMN, or ArchiMate. Study their principles, tools, and best practices, and practice applying them to real-world scenarios. Understanding these frameworks in depth will enhance your ability to design and manage business architectures effectively.

Change Management Simulations

Participate in change management simulations where you lead an organisation through a business process transformation. These simulations help you develop the skills necessary to manage resistance, communicate effectively, and ensure the successful adoption of changes.

The Technology Architect

The Technology Architect plays a pivotal role in designing and managing the underlying technology infrastructure that supports an organisation's applications, data, and operations. This role requires a deep understanding of various technology domains, from networking and cloud computing to security and data management. The Technology Architect ensures that the organisation's IT infrastructure is robust, scalable, and aligned with business objectives. This chapter will explore the skills necessary for a Technology Architect, how they perform their job, best practices for success, and some suggested learning exercises to help develop and refine these skills.

Skills Necessary for a Technology Architect

To excel as a Technology Architect, a combination of technical expertise, strategic thinking, and communication skills is essential. The following are key skills required for the role:

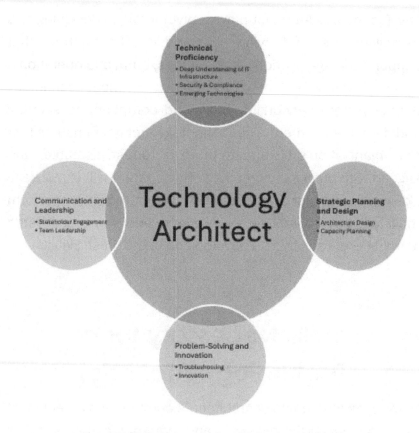

Figure 17: Skills Necessary for a Technology Architect

Technical Proficiency

Technical proficiency is a cornerstone of the Technology Architect's role, requiring a deep and comprehensive understanding of IT infrastructure, including servers, networks, storage, virtualisation, and cloud technologies. This expertise is crucial for designing systems that are not only efficient and reliable but also scalable enough to support the organisation's current and future needs. In addition to technical knowledge, a strong grasp of security principles, practices, and regulatory requirements is essential. The Technology Architect must ensure that all infrastructure components are secure, compliant with industry standards, and capable of protecting the organisation's data and systems from various threats. Moreover, staying abreast of emerging technologies, such as containerisation, microservices, and edge computing, is vital for keeping the organisation's infrastructure both innovative and competitive. The ability to evaluate, adopt, and integrate new technologies into the existing architecture is a key skill that enables the Technology Architect to drive continuous improvement and maintain a cutting-edge infrastructure.

Strategic Planning and Design

The Technology Architect must possess a high level of skill in designing architectures that are closely aligned with the organisation's strategic goals. This responsibility involves creating detailed blueprints for the IT infrastructure that support the business objectives, ensuring that all technology investments are in line with the long-term strategies of the organisation. By aligning the architecture with the strategic vision, the Technology Architect plays a key role in driving the organisation's growth and ensuring that IT systems are "future-proof". Additionally, capacity planning is a critical aspect of this role. The Technology Architect must anticipate the organisation's future needs and design systems that can scale accordingly. This includes ensuring that the infrastructure is flexible enough to handle growth and adapt to changes in demand, thus maintaining performance and reliability as the organisation evolves.

Problem-Solving and Innovation

Strong problem-solving skills are essential for a Technology Architect, particularly when it comes to identifying and resolving issues within the IT infrastructure. This includes diagnosing system failures, performance bottlenecks, and security vulnerabilities—challenges that require a methodical and analytical approach to ensure swift resolution. Beyond troubleshooting, the ability to think creatively and propose innovative solutions is crucial. The Technology Architect must continuously seek out and leverage new technologies and approaches to improve infrastructure efficiency, reduce operational costs, and enhance overall performance. Innovation in this context is not just about adopting the latest technologies but about applying them in ways that deliver tangible benefits to the organisation.

Communication and Leadership

Effective communication with stakeholders is a cornerstone of success for a Technology Architect. This includes engaging with business leaders, IT teams, and external vendors, all of whom play a role in the successful implementation of the IT architecture. The Technology Architect must be able to translate complex technical concepts into language that non-technical stakeholders can understand, which is crucial for securing support and ensuring that everyone is aligned with the project goals. In addition to communication, strong leadership skills are required, as the Technology Architect often leads or collaborates with cross-functional teams. Guiding these teams through the design and implementation of infrastructure projects requires not only technical expertise but also the ability to manage people and resources effectively, ensuring that goals are met on time and within budget.

How a Technology Architect Performs Their Job

The role of a Technology Architect is dynamic and involves a range of activities, from strategic planning to hands-on implementation. Here's how a Technology Architect typically performs their job:

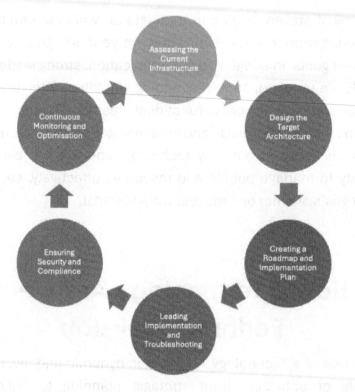

Figure 18: Typical Technology Architect job flow

Assessing the Current Infrastructure

The first step in the Technology Architect's process is to assess the current state of the organisation's IT infrastructure. This involves conducting a thorough review of existing systems, identifying strengths and weaknesses, and understanding how well the infrastructure supports business objectives. The Technology Architect maps out the technology landscape, including servers, networks, storage, and cloud environments, to gain a comprehensive understanding of the current setup.

168

Designing the Target Architecture

Based on the assessment, the Technology Architect develops a vision for the target architecture that aligns with the organisation's strategic goals. This involves creating detailed architectural designs that outline the future state of the IT infrastructure, including any new technologies, systems, or configurations that need to be implemented. The design phase also includes capacity planning, ensuring that the architecture can scale to meet future demands.

Creating a Roadmap and Implementation Plan

Once the target architecture is defined, the Technology Architect develops a roadmap that outlines the steps required to transition from the current state to the desired future state. This roadmap includes key milestones, timelines, and resource allocation. The Technology Architect also works closely with project managers and IT teams to develop detailed implementation plans, which include tasks such as system configuration, testing, and deployment.

Leading Implementation and Troubleshooting

During the implementation phase, the Technology Architect takes on a leadership role, overseeing the execution of the roadmap and providing guidance to the IT teams. The architect ensures that the implementation stays on track and addresses any issues that arise. Troubleshooting is a key part of this role, as the Technology Architect must be prepared to identify and resolve technical challenges that could impact the success of the project.

Ensuring Security and Compliance

The Technology Architect is responsible for ensuring that the infrastructure is secure and compliant with industry regulations. This involves implementing security controls, monitoring systems for vulnerabilities, and ensuring that all components meet regulatory requirements. The Technology Architect also works closely with security teams to conduct audits and assessments, ensuring that the infrastructure remains resilient against threats.

Continuous Monitoring and Optimisation

After the infrastructure is implemented, the Technology Architect continuously monitors its performance to ensure that it meets the organisation's needs. This involves analysing performance metrics, identifying areas for improvement, and making adjustments to optimise efficiency and reliability. The Technology Architect also stays informed about emerging technologies and trends, evaluating their potential impact on the organisation and integrating them into the architecture as needed.

Best Practices for Success as a Technology Architect

To be successful as a Technology Architect, certain best practices should be followed:

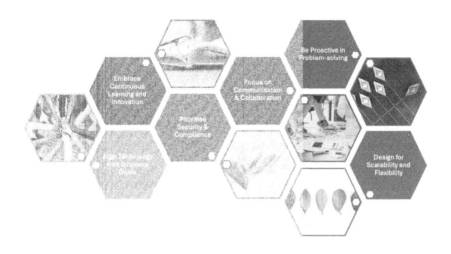

Figure 19: Best Practices for Success as a Technology Architect

Align Technology Architecture with Business Goals

Always ensure that the technology architecture is closely aligned with the organisation's strategic goals. This alignment is critical for demonstrating the value of IT investments and ensuring that the infrastructure supports the organisation's long-term objectives.

Prioritise Security and Compliance

Security and compliance should be top priorities in the design and management of the IT infrastructure. Implement robust security measures, stay informed about regulatory requirements, and conduct regular audits to ensure that the infrastructure is secure and compliant.

Embrace Continuous Learning and Innovation

The technology landscape is constantly evolving, and successful Technology Architects are those who commit to continuous learning. Stay current with the latest trends, tools, and methodologies in technology, and be open to adopting new technologies that can improve infrastructure performance and efficiency.

Focus on Communication and Collaboration

Strong communication and collaboration skills are essential for success as a Technology Architect. Foster an environment of open communication, where ideas can be shared freely, and feedback is encouraged. Collaborate with business units, IT teams, and external vendors to ensure that everyone is working towards common goals.

Be Proactive in Problem-Solving

Anticipate potential issues before they arise and develop strategies to address them proactively. This includes conducting thorough risk assessments, planning for contingencies, and being prepared to troubleshoot problems as they occur.

Design for Scalability and Flexibility

Design technology architectures that are scalable and adaptable to change. The ability to pivot and respond quickly to new business requirements, technological advancements, or market changes is essential for maintaining the relevance and effectiveness of the technology infrastructure.

Learning Exercises to Develop Technology Architecture Skills

To develop and refine the skills necessary for success as a Technology Architect, consider the following learning exercises:

Case Study Analysis

Analyse case studies of successful and unsuccessful technology architecture initiatives. Identify the key factors that contributed to their outcomes, and reflect on how you would approach similar challenges. This exercise will help you develop critical thinking and problem-solving skills.

Technology Simulation Exercises

Participate in simulation exercises where you are tasked with designing and implementing a technology architecture for a hypothetical organisation. These simulations can help you apply theoretical knowledge in a practical setting and improve your decision-making and strategic planning skills.

Security and Compliance Workshops

Attend workshops focused on security and compliance in IT architecture. These workshops provide hands-on experience with implementing security controls, conducting audits, and ensuring that infrastructure components meet regulatory requirements.

Emerging Technology Research

Conduct research on emerging technologies and evaluate their potential impact on IT infrastructure. This exercise will help you stay informed about the latest trends and technologies, and develop the ability to integrate them into your architecture.

Cross-Functional Collaboration Projects

Engage in cross-functional projects where you collaborate with different business units, IT teams, and external vendors. This exercise will help you improve your communication, collaboration, and stakeholder management skills, ensuring that you can lead successful technology architecture initiatives.

The Information Architect

The Information Architect plays a vital role in managing and structuring an organisation's data and information assets. Their work is critical in ensuring that data is organised, accessible, and leveraged effectively to support business objectives. Information Architects design the frameworks that govern how data is stored, accessed, and utilised across the organisation, bridging the gap between IT infrastructure and business needs. This chapter explores the skills necessary for an Information Architect, how they perform their job, best practices for success, and some suggested learning exercises to help develop and refine these skills.

Skills Necessary for an Information Architect

To be effective in their role, an Information Architect must possess a unique combination of technical expertise, analytical thinking, and communication skills. The following are key skills required for the role:

Figure 20: Skills Necessary for an Information Architect

Data Management and Modelling

A deep understanding of data modelling techniques is essential for an Information Architect. This involves the ability to create conceptual, logical, and physical data models that accurately represent the organisation's data structures. Mastery of modelling tools such as ERwin, Visio, or UML is

177

crucial for designing databases and information systems that are both efficient and scalable. These models serve as the blueprint for how data is stored, accessed, and managed across the organisation, ensuring that the data architecture supports business objectives effectively.

In addition to data modelling, knowledge of data governance principles is vital for an Information Architect. They must establish and enforce data governance frameworks that ensure data quality, consistency, and security. This includes setting policies for data usage, access, and retention, ensuring compliance with industry standards and regulations. Effective data governance helps maintain the integrity of data assets and supports the organisation's strategic goals.

Technical Proficiency

The Information Architect must possess a strong command of various database technologies to design systems that meet the specific needs of the organisation. This includes expertise in relational databases like SQL Server and Oracle, as well as NoSQL databases such as MongoDB and Cassandra. This technical knowledge allows the Information Architect to choose the right database solutions for different types of data, whether structured or unstructured.

Additionally, proficiency in data integration tools and techniques is necessary for ensuring seamless data flow across different systems. The Information Architect should be skilled in ETL (Extract, Transform, Load) processes, APIs, and middleware solutions that facilitate data exchange between applications and databases. This ensures that data is consistent, accurate, and readily available to support business processes and decision-making.

Analytical and Problem-Solving Skills

The ability to analyse large datasets and extract meaningful insights is critical for an Information Architect. They must be able to identify trends, correlations, and patterns in data that can inform business decisions and drive strategy. Familiarity with data analysis tools like SQL, Python, or R is advantageous, as these tools help in manipulating and interpreting data efficiently.

Beyond analysis, Information Architects must also be adept at identifying and resolving data-related issues, such as data redundancy, inconsistency, and security vulnerabilities. This requires a keen analytical mind and the ability to think critically about complex data challenges. Effective problem-solving ensures that the data architecture remains robust, reliable, and aligned with the organisation's goals.

Communication and Collaboration

Effective communication with stakeholders is crucial for the success of an Information Architect. This includes engaging with business leaders, data scientists, and IT teams to ensure that the data architecture aligns with business goals. The Information Architect must be able to translate complex technical concepts into language that non-technical stakeholders can understand, facilitating better decision-making and alignment.

Collaboration is equally important, as the Information Architect often works closely with various teams across the organisation, including data governance, IT, and business analytics teams. Strong collaboration skills are essential for ensuring that data strategies are implemented effectively and that data assets are used optimally. By fostering collaboration and maintaining open lines of communication, the Information Architect helps to create a cohesive and integrated data environment that supports the organisation's strategic objectives.

How an Information Architect Performs Their Job

The role of an Information Architect is dynamic and involves a range of activities, from data modelling to stakeholder engagement. Here's how an Information Architect typically performs their job:

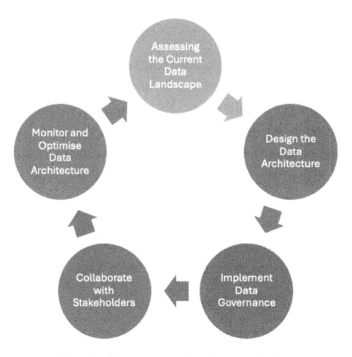

Figure 21: Typical Information Architect job flow

Assessing the Current Data Landscape

The first step for an Information Architect is to assess the current state of the organisation's data architecture. This involves conducting a thorough review of existing databases, data flows, and storage systems. The Information Architect identifies strengths and weaknesses in the current setup and determines how well the existing architecture supports business objectives. This assessment provides the foundation for developing a more efficient and scalable data architecture.

181

Designing the Data Architecture

Based on the assessment, the Information Architect designs a comprehensive data architecture that aligns with the organisation's strategic goals. This involves creating detailed data models that define how data is structured, stored, and accessed across the organisation. The Information Architect also designs data integration frameworks that ensure seamless data flow between different systems and applications. This phase includes selecting the appropriate database technologies, defining data governance policies, and ensuring that the architecture is scalable to meet future needs.

Implementing Data Governance

Implementing data governance is a critical aspect of the Information Architect's role. This involves establishing policies and procedures for data management, including data quality standards, access controls, and retention policies. The Information Architect ensures that these governance frameworks are adhered to across the organisation, maintaining the integrity and security of data assets. This governance structure also ensures compliance with industry regulations and standards, protecting the organisation from potential legal and operational risks.

Collaborating with Stakeholders

Throughout the process, the Information Architect engages with stakeholders across the organisation to gather input, build consensus, and ensure alignment with business goals. This involves facilitating workshops, leading discussions, and translating technical concepts into business-friendly language. Effective stakeholder engagement is key to ensuring that the data architecture meets the needs of the organisation and that data strategies are implemented successfully.

Monitoring and Optimising Data Architecture

After implementing the data architecture, the Information Architect continuously monitors its performance to ensure that it meets the organisation's needs. This involves analysing data usage patterns, identifying areas for improvement, and making adjustments to optimise efficiency and reliability. The Information Architect also stays informed about emerging data technologies and trends, evaluating their potential impact on the organisation and integrating them into the architecture as needed.

Best Practices for Success as an Information Architect

To be successful as an Information Architect, certain best practices should be followed:

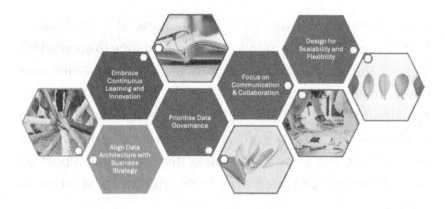

Figure 22: Best Practices for Success as an Information Architect

Align Data Architecture with Business Strategy

Always ensure that the data architecture is closely aligned with the organisation's strategic goals. This alignment is critical for demonstrating the value of data assets and ensuring that the architecture supports the organisation's long-term objectives.

Prioritise Data Governance

Data governance should be a top priority in the design and management of data architecture. Implement robust data governance frameworks, enforce data quality standards, and ensure compliance with industry regulations. This approach ensures the integrity and security of the organisation's data assets.

Embrace Continuous Learning and Innovation

The data landscape is constantly evolving, and successful Information Architects are those who commit to continuous learning. Stay current with the latest trends, tools, and methodologies in data management and be open to adopting new technologies that can improve data architecture and enhance business outcomes.

Focus on Communication and Collaboration

Strong communication and collaboration skills are essential for success as an Information Architect. Foster an environment of open communication, where ideas can be shared freely, and feedback is encouraged. Collaborate with business units, IT teams, and data governance teams to ensure that everyone is working towards common goals.

Design for Scalability and Flexibility

Design data architectures that are scalable and adaptable to change. The ability to pivot and respond quickly to new business requirements, technological advancements, or data challenges is essential for maintaining the relevance and effectiveness of the data architecture.

Learning Exercises to Develop Information Architecture Skills

To develop and refine the skills necessary for success as an Information Architect, consider the following learning exercises:

Data Modelling Workshops

Participate in or lead workshops focused on data modelling techniques. Practice creating conceptual, logical, and physical data models using tools like ERwin or Visio. This exercise will help you develop a deeper understanding of data structures and improve your ability to design efficient and scalable databases.

Data Governance Simulations

Engage in simulations where you implement data governance frameworks for a hypothetical organisation. This exercise will help you understand the complexities of data governance, including setting policies for data quality, access, and retention, and ensuring compliance with industry standards.

Case Study Analysis

Analyse case studies of successful and unsuccessful data architecture initiatives. Identify the key factors that contributed to their outcomes, and reflect on how you would approach similar challenges. This exercise will help you develop critical thinking and problem-solving skills.

Database Technology Research

Conduct research on various database technologies, both relational and NoSQL. Evaluate their strengths, weaknesses, and use cases, and practice applying them to real-world scenarios. This exercise will help you stay informed about the latest database trends and improve your technical proficiency.

Cross-Functional Collaboration Projects

Participate in cross-functional projects where you collaborate with different business units, IT teams, and data governance teams. This exercise will help you improve your communication, collaboration, and stakeholder management skills, ensuring that you can lead successful data architecture initiatives.

The Security Architect

In today's digital landscape, where cyber threats are increasingly sophisticated and prevalent, the role of the Security Architect is more critical than ever. The Security Architect is responsible for designing, implementing, and managing the organisation's security architecture, ensuring that all systems, data, and networks are protected against potential threats. This role requires a deep understanding of security principles, technologies, and best practices to safeguard the organisation's assets while aligning with its business objectives. This chapter explores the skills necessary for a Security Architect, how they perform their job, best practices for success, and suggested learning exercises to help develop and refine these skills.

Skills Necessary for a Security Architect

To be effective in their role, a Security Architect must possess a diverse set of technical and analytical skills, coupled with strong strategic thinking and communication abilities. The following are key skills required for the role:

Figure 23: Skills Necessary for a Security Architect

Technical Proficiency

A comprehensive understanding of cybersecurity principles, practices, and technologies is essential for a Security Architect. This expertise includes deep knowledge of encryption techniques, firewalls, intrusion detection systems, secure coding practices, and threat modelling. The Security Architect must be well-versed in these areas to effectively protect the organisation against evolving threats. Additionally, staying up-to-date with the latest developments in cybersecurity is crucial for ensuring that the organisation's defences are robust and responsive to new challenges.

Proficiency in network security is also critical for a Security Architect. They must be skilled in designing and managing secure networks, which includes implementing Zero-Trust Network Access (ZTNA), network segmentation, and secure access controls. Understanding how to protect the network infrastructure from various types of attacks is a key component of this role, as it helps to ensure the overall security and integrity of the organisation's IT environment.

Risk Management and Compliance

The ability to conduct thorough risk assessments is a critical skill for a Security Architect. This involves identifying potential vulnerabilities within the organisation's IT systems, evaluating the likelihood and impact of various threats, and prioritising risks based on their potential impact on the organisation. The Security Architect must develop and implement strategies to mitigate these risks effectively, ensuring that the organisation is protected against potential security breaches.

Additionally, a strong understanding of regulatory requirements and industry standards, such as Europe's GDPR, Singapore's PDPA, healthcare industry's HIPAA, and other standards like ISO/IEC 27001, is essential. The Security Architect must ensure that the organisation's security architecture complies with these regulations and standards, protecting the organisation from legal and financial penalties while maintaining high standards of data protection and privacy.

Analytical and Problem-Solving Skills

The Security Architect must be adept at analysing potential threats and developing proactive strategies to address them. This involves staying informed about the latest cyber threats and understanding how they could impact the organisation. The ability to think critically and anticipate potential security challenges is vital for preventing security breaches and minimising their impact.

In the event of a security breach, the Security Architect must be able to respond quickly and effectively. This includes identifying the source of the breach, containing the threat, and implementing measures to prevent future incidents. Strong problem-solving skills are essential for managing security incidents, minimising their impact on the organisation, and ensuring that normal operations can be restored as quickly as possible.

Strategic Planning and Design

The Security Architect is responsible for designing a comprehensive security architecture that aligns with the organisation's business objectives. This involves creating security frameworks, selecting appropriate security technologies, and integrating security into all aspects of the organisation's IT infrastructure. The goal is to create a cohesive and resilient security architecture that supports the organisation's strategic goals while providing robust protection against threats.

Additionally, the Security Architect must continuously assess and improve the organisation's security posture. This involves monitoring security trends, evaluating the effectiveness of existing security measures, and implementing new strategies to enhance protection. A proactive approach to security is essential for staying ahead of potential threats and ensuring that the organisation remains secure in an ever-changing threat landscape.

Communication and Collaboration

Effective communication with stakeholders, including executives, IT teams, and external partners, is crucial for a Security Architect. The ability to articulate complex security concepts in a way that non-technical stakeholders can understand is key to securing buy-in and ensuring that security measures are implemented effectively across the organisation.

Additionally, the Security Architect often works closely with cross-functional teams, including IT, legal, and compliance departments. Strong collaboration skills are necessary for coordinating security efforts across the organisation and ensuring that all teams are aligned with the security strategy. This collaborative approach helps to create a unified and effective security posture that protects the organisation from threats while supporting its overall business objectives.

How a Security Architect Performs Their Job

The Security Architect's role is dynamic and involves a range of activities, from strategic planning to hands-on implementation. Here's how a Security Architect typically performs their job:

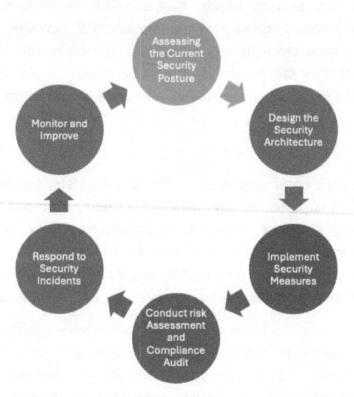

Figure 24: Typical Security Architect job flow

Assessing the Current Security Posture

The first step in the Security Architect's process is to assess the organisation's current security posture. This involves conducting a thorough review of existing security measures, identifying vulnerabilities, and evaluating how well the current security architecture aligns with the organisation's risk tolerance and business objectives. The Security Architect uses this assessment to develop a baseline understanding of the organisation's security needs.

Designing the Security Architecture

Based on the assessment, the Security Architect designs a comprehensive security architecture that aligns with the organisation's strategic goals. This involves selecting and implementing security technologies, such as firewalls, intrusion detection systems, and encryption protocols, that protect the organisation's data and systems. The Security Architect also designs secure network architectures, implements access controls, and ensures that all aspects of the organisation's IT infrastructure are protected against potential threats.

Implementing Security Measures

Once the security architecture is designed, the Security Architect oversees the implementation of security measures across the organisation. This involves configuring security technologies, setting up monitoring systems, and ensuring that all employees are trained in security best practices. The

Security Architect works closely with IT teams to integrate security into all aspects of the organisation's operations, from application development to network management.

Conducting Risk Assessments and Compliance Audits

The Security Architect is responsible for ensuring that regular risk assessments and compliance audits are conducted to ensure that the organisation's security measures are effective and compliant with regulatory requirements. This involves identifying new vulnerabilities, evaluating the effectiveness of existing security controls, and making recommendations for improvement. The Security Architect also ensures that the organisation stays up-to-date with changes in regulations and industry standards.

Responding to Security Incidents

In the event of a security breach, the Security Architect plays a key role in incident response. This includes working with the incident responses team to identify the source of the breach, containing the threat, and designing and implementing measures to prevent future incidents. The Security Architect assist in coordination with IT teams, legal departments, and external partners to manage the incident and minimise its impact on the organisation. After the incident is resolved, the Security Architect conducts a post-incident review to identify lessons learned and improve the organisation's security posture.

Continuous Monitoring and Improvement

The Security Architect continuously monitors the organisation's security environment to detect potential threats and assess the effectiveness of security measures. This involves analysing security logs, conducting penetration tests, and staying informed about the latest cybersecurity trends. The Security Architect uses this information to make ongoing improvements to the security architecture, ensuring that the organisation remains protected against emerging threats.

Best Practices for Success as a Security Architect

To be successful as a Security Architect, certain best practices should be followed:

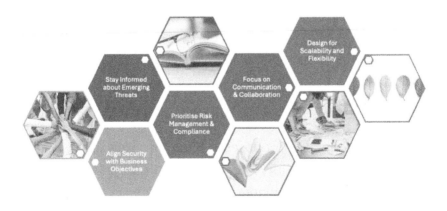

Figure 25: Best Practices for Success as a Security Architect

Align Security with Business Objectives

Always ensure that the security architecture is closely aligned with the organisation's strategic goals. This alignment is critical for demonstrating the value of security investments and ensuring that security measures support the organisation's long-term objectives.

Prioritise Risk Management and Compliance

Risk management and compliance should be top priorities in the design and management of security architecture. Conduct regular risk assessments, stay informed about regulatory requirements, and ensure that the organisation's security measures are compliant with industry standards.

Stay Informed About Emerging Threats

The cybersecurity landscape is constantly evolving, and successful Security Architects are those who commit to continuous learning. Stay current with the latest cyber threats, technologies, and best practices, and be proactive in implementing new security measures to protect the organisation.

Focus on Communication and Collaboration

Strong communication and collaboration skills are essential for success as a Security Architect. Foster an environment of open communication, where security concerns can be raised and addressed promptly. Collaborate with IT teams, legal departments, and external partners to ensure that everyone is working towards common security goals.

Design for Scalability and Flexibility

Design security architectures that are scalable and adaptable to change. The ability to pivot and respond quickly to new threats, technological advancements, or regulatory changes is essential for maintaining the relevance and effectiveness of the security architecture.

Learning Exercises to Develop Security Architecture Skills

To develop and refine the skills necessary for success as a Security Architect, consider the following learning exercises:

Cybersecurity Certification Courses

Enrol in cybersecurity certification courses such as Certified Information Systems Security Professional (CISSP), Certified Information Security Manager (CISM), or Sherwood Applied Business Security Architecture (SABSA). These courses provide in-depth knowledge of cybersecurity principles, practices, and technologies, helping you build a strong foundation in security architecture.

Risk Assessment Simulations

Participate in simulations where you conduct risk assessments for a hypothetical organisation. This exercise will help you develop the skills needed to identify vulnerabilities, evaluate risks, and prioritise security measures based on their potential impact.

Compliance Audits

Conduct mock compliance audits for your organisation or a hypothetical scenario. This exercise will help you understand the complexities of regulatory requirements, evaluate your organisation's compliance posture, and identify areas for improvement.

Threat Modelling Workshops

Engage in threat modelling workshops where you identify potential threats to a system, evaluate their likelihood and impact, and develop strategies to mitigate them. This exercise will help you improve your ability to anticipate security challenges and design proactive solutions.

Cross-Functional Security Projects:

Participate in cross-functional projects where you collaborate with IT, legal, and compliance teams to develop and implement security measures. This exercise will help you improve your communication, collaboration, and stakeholder management skills, ensuring that you can lead successful security architecture initiatives.

The Integration Architect

The role of the Integration Architect is **critical in modern** enterprises where multiple systems, applications, and data sources must work together seamlessly to support business operations. An Integration Architect is responsible for designing and managing the integration of various systems, ensuring that they communicate effectively and function as a unified whole. This role requires a deep understanding of both the technical and business aspects of system integration, as well as the ability to navigate complex IT environments. This chapter explores the skills necessary for an Integration Architect, how they perform their job, best practices for success, and suggested learning exercises to help develop and refine these skills.

Skills Necessary for an Integration Architect

To excel as an Integration Architect, a combination of technical expertise, problem-solving abilities, and strong communication skills is essential. The following are key skills required for the role:

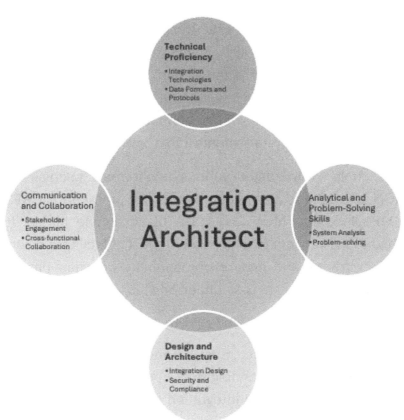

Figure 26: Skills Necessary for an Integration Architect

Technical Proficiency

A deep understanding of integration technologies is crucial for an Integration Architect. This includes expertise in Enterprise Service Buses (ESBs), API management platforms, middleware, and microservices architecture. These technologies are foundational for enabling different systems to communicate

203

and work together seamlessly. The Integration Architect must be proficient in tools like MuleSoft, Dell Boomi, Apache Kafka/Camel, or IBM Integration Bus, which are essential for designing and managing integrations across various systems. These tools facilitate the orchestration of data flow and the integration of disparate systems into a cohesive whole.

Additionally, knowledge of various data formats, such as XML, JSON, and CSV, as well as communication protocols like REST, SOAP, JMS, and MQTT, is vital. This expertise allows the Integration Architect to design solutions that facilitate smooth data exchange and ensure compatibility between different systems, regardless of their underlying technologies.

Analytical and Problem-Solving Skills

The Integration Architect must be adept at system analysis, particularly in understanding how complex systems interact and identifying potential integration challenges. This involves mapping out data flows, identifying dependencies, and assessing how changes in one system might impact others. By thoroughly analysing these interactions, the Integration Architect can design integrations that are both efficient and resilient.

Effective problem-solving skills are also essential for addressing integration issues that may arise, such as data mismatches, latency problems, or communication breakdowns between systems. The Integration Architect must be able to diagnose these issues quickly and implement solutions that minimise disruption to business operations, ensuring that integrations function smoothly and effectively support business processes.

Design and Architecture

The Integration Architect is responsible for designing integration solutions that are scalable, flexible, and aligned with the organisation's business objectives. This involves creating detailed integration blueprints that outline how different systems will connect and communicate. The Integration Architect must select appropriate technologies and define data flow and transformation processes that ensure the integration is robust and adaptable to future changes.

Additionally, ensuring that integration solutions are secure and compliant with industry regulations is a key responsibility. The Integration Architect must design architectures that protect data as it moves between systems, implementing measures such as encryption, authentication, and access control to safeguard sensitive information and ensure compliance with regulatory requirements.

Communication and Collaboration

Effective communication with stakeholders is crucial for a successful Integration Architect. This includes engaging with business leaders, IT teams, and external vendors to ensure that everyone involved understands the integration strategy and its importance to the organisation. The Integration Architect must be able to explain complex technical concepts in a way that non-technical stakeholders can understand, ensuring alignment with business goals and securing support for integration projects.

Additionally, cross-functional collaboration is essential, as the Integration Architect often works closely with various teams across the organisation, including developers, data architects, and network engineers. Strong collaboration skills are necessary to ensure that integration solutions are implemented successfully and that all teams are aligned with the overall strategy, leading to cohesive and effective integrations that support the organisation's objectives.

How an Integration Architect Performs Their Job

The Integration Architect's role involves a wide range of activities, from strategic planning to hands-on implementation. Here's how an Integration Architect typically performs their job:

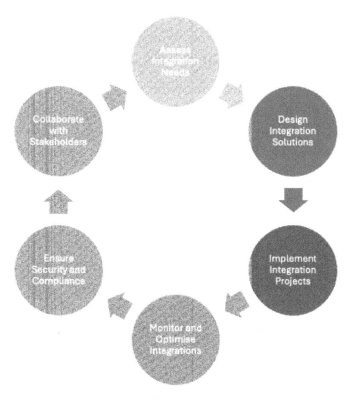

Figure 27: Typical Integration Architect job flow

Assessing Integration Needs

The first step for an Integration Architect is to assess the organisation's current systems and identify integration needs. This involves conducting a thorough analysis of existing systems, understanding how they interact, and identifying any gaps or inefficiencies. The Integration Architect works closely with stakeholders to understand their requirements and ensure that the integration strategy aligns with business goals.

Designing Integration Solutions

Based on the assessment, the Integration Architect designs integration solutions that facilitate seamless communication between systems. This involves creating detailed integration blueprints that outline data flows, transformation processes, and communication protocols. The Integration Architect selects the appropriate integration technologies and ensures that the design is scalable, secure, and aligned with the organisation's strategic objectives.

Implementing Integration Projects

Once the integration solutions are designed, the Integration Architect oversees their implementation. This involves configuring integration platforms, setting up data transformation rules, and ensuring that all systems are properly connected. The Integration Architect works closely with development and IT teams to implement the integrations, troubleshoot any issues that arise, and ensure that the solutions are deployed successfully.

Monitoring and Optimising Integrations

After the integration solutions are implemented, the Integration Architect continuously monitors their performance to ensure that they are functioning as expected. This involves tracking data flows, identifying any bottlenecks or latency issues, and making adjustments to optimise performance. The Integration Architect also stays informed about new technologies and trends in integration, evaluating their potential impact on the organisation and incorporating them into the architecture as needed.

Ensuring Security and Compliance

The Integration Architect is responsible for ensuring that all integration solutions are secure and compliant with industry regulations. This involves implementing encryption, authentication, and access control measures to protect data as it moves between systems. The Integration Architect also conducts regular audits to ensure that the integrations remain compliant with changing regulations and industry standards.

Collaborating with Stakeholders

Throughout the process, the Integration Architect engages with stakeholders across the organisation to gather input, build consensus, and ensure alignment with business goals. This involves facilitating meetings, leading discussions, and providing regular updates on the progress of integration projects. Effective stakeholder engagement is key to ensuring that integration solutions meet the needs of the organisation and are implemented successfully.

Best Practices for Success as an Integration Architect

To be successful as an Integration Architect, certain best practices should be followed:

Figure 28: Best Practices for Success as an Integration Architect

Align Integration Solutions with Business Objectives

Always ensure that integration solutions are closely aligned with the organisation's strategic goals. This alignment is critical for demonstrating the value of integration projects and ensuring that they support the organisation's long-term objectives.

Prioritise Security and Compliance:

Security and compliance should be top priorities in the design and management of integration solutions. Implement robust security measures, stay informed about regulatory requirements, and conduct regular audits to ensure that integrations are secure and compliant.

Embrace Continuous Learning and Innovation:

The integration landscape is constantly evolving, and successful Integration Architects are those who commit to continuous learning. Stay current with the latest integration technologies, tools, and methodologies, and be open to adopting new approaches that can improve integration performance and efficiency.

Focus on Communication and Collaboration

Strong communication and collaboration skills are essential for success as an Integration Architect. Foster an environment of open communication, where ideas can be shared freely, and feedback is encouraged. Collaborate with business units, IT teams, and external vendors to ensure that everyone is working towards common goals.

Design for Scalability and Flexibility:

Design integration solutions that are scalable and adaptable to change. The ability to pivot and respond quickly to new business requirements, technological advancements, or integration challenges is essential for maintaining the relevance and effectiveness of the integration architecture.

Learning Exercises to Develop Integration Architecture Skills

To develop and refine the skills necessary for success as an Integration Architect, consider the following learning exercises:

Integration Technology Workshops

Participate in or lead workshops focused on integration technologies, such as ESBs, API management platforms, and microservices architecture. Practice configuring integration platforms and designing integration solutions for various use cases.

Case Study Analysis

Analyse case studies of successful and unsuccessful integration projects. Identify the key factors that contributed to their outcomes, and reflect on how you would approach similar challenges. This exercise will help you develop critical thinking and problem-solving skills.

Security and Compliance Audits

Conduct mock security and compliance audits for integration solutions. This exercise will help you understand the complexities of securing integrations and ensuring compliance with industry regulations.

Simulation Exercises

Engage in simulation exercises where you are tasked with designing and implementing an integration architecture for a hypothetical organisation. These simulations can help you apply theoretical knowledge in a practical setting and improve your decision-making and strategic planning skills.

Cross-Functional Collaboration Projects

Participate in cross-functional projects where you collaborate with different business units, IT teams, and external vendors. This exercise will help you improve your communication, collaboration, and stakeholder management skills, ensuring that you can lead successful integration architecture initiatives.

The Solutions Architect

A Solutions Architect is a critical role in any organisation, serving as the bridge between business needs and technological solutions. The primary responsibility of a Solutions Architect is to design comprehensive, high-quality, and scalable solutions that address specific business challenges while aligning with the overall strategy and architecture of the organisation. This chapter will explore the skills necessary for a Solutions Architect, how they perform their job, best practices for success, and suggested learning exercises to help develop and refine these skills.

Skills Necessary for a Solutions Architect

To excel as a Solutions Architect, a blend of technical expertise, business acumen, and strong interpersonal skills is essential. The following are key skills required for the role:

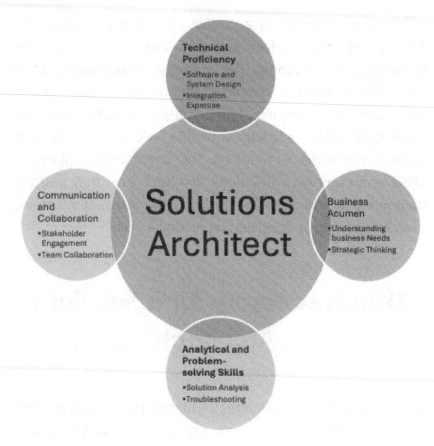

Figure 29: Skills Necessary for a Solutions Architect

Technical Proficiency

A deep understanding of software development processes, system architecture, and design patterns is crucial for a Solutions Architect. They must be proficient in designing software solutions that are robust, scalable, and maintainable, ensuring that these solutions can withstand future growth and changes. This proficiency includes knowledge of various programming languages, development frameworks, and cloud platforms such as Amazon Web Services (AWS), Microsoft Azure, or Google Cloud Platform (GCP), all of which are essential for building modern, resilient applications.

Additionally, Solutions Architects need to be skilled in integrating various systems and technologies to ensure that the solution works seamlessly within the existing IT environment. This expertise involves understanding APIs, middleware, and integration patterns that enable different systems to communicate effectively, ensuring that the entire IT ecosystem operates cohesively.

Business Acumen

A Solutions Architect must have a solid grasp of the organisation's business goals, processes, and challenges. This understanding is critical for designing solutions that not only meet technical requirements but also deliver tangible business value. By aligning technical solutions with business objectives, the Solutions Architect ensures that the technology supports and enhances the organisation's strategic goals. They must be able to translate business requirements into technical specifications that developers can implement, ensuring that the solution is both functional and aligned with business needs.

Moreover, strategic thinking is essential, as Solutions Architects must consider how their designs will contribute to the organisation's long-term success. They must think strategically about how technology can drive business growth, improve efficiency, and create competitive advantages, ensuring that the solutions they design are future-proof and aligned with the broader business strategy.

Analytical and Problem-Solving Skills

Solutions Architects are responsible for analysing various options and selecting the best approach to meet business and technical requirements. This involves evaluating the feasibility, risks, and benefits of different solutions and making informed decisions that balance short-term needs with long-term goals. The ability to analyse complex problems and identify the most effective solutions is critical for ensuring that the final design meets all necessary criteria.

Additionally, when issues arise during the design or implementation of a solution, the Solutions Architect must be adept at diagnosing the problem and identifying the root cause. Strong problem-solving skills are essential for quickly resolving issues and ensuring that the solution remains on track, minimising disruptions and ensuring successful project outcomes.

Communication and Collaboration

Effective communication with stakeholders is critical for a Solutions Architect. This includes working closely with business leaders, project managers, developers, and external vendors to gather requirements, provide updates, and ensure that everyone is aligned with the project's goals. The ability to translate complex technical concepts into understandable terms is key to securing buy-in and support from all stakeholders.

Additionally, Solutions Architects often work closely with cross-functional teams, including developers, testers, and IT operations. Strong collaboration skills are necessary to ensure that all team members are working towards a common goal and that the solution is delivered on time and within budget. By fostering a collaborative environment, the Solutions Architect ensures that the project benefits from diverse expertise and that all aspects of the solution are considered and addressed effectively.

How a Solutions Architect Performs Their Job

The Solutions Architect's role involves a wide range of activities, from gathering requirements to overseeing the implementation of the solution. Here's how a Solutions Architect typically performs their job:

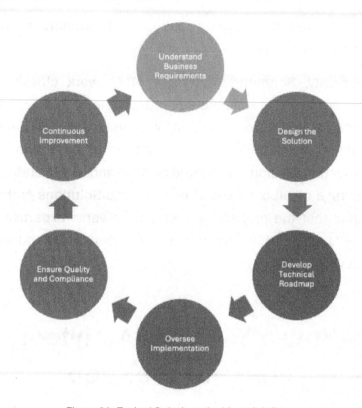

Figure 30: Typical Solutions Architect job flow

Understanding Business Requirements

The first step in the Solutions Architect's process is to engage with stakeholders to understand the business requirements. This involves conducting meetings and workshops to gather information about the organisation's needs, challenges, and goals. The Solutions Architect must be able to translate these business requirements into technical specifications that guide the design of the solution.

Designing the Solution

Based on the gathered requirements, the Solutions Architect designs a comprehensive solution that addresses the business challenges while aligning with the organisation's strategic goals. This involves creating high-level architecture diagrams, selecting the appropriate technologies, and defining the components and interactions of the system. The Solutions Architect must ensure that the solution is scalable, secure, and maintainable, considering both current and future needs.

Developing a Technical Roadmap

Once the solution design is complete, the Solutions Architect creates a technical roadmap that outlines the steps required to implement the solution. This roadmap includes key milestones, timelines, and resource allocation, ensuring that the project stays on track. The Solutions Architect works closely with project managers and development teams to ensure that the roadmap is feasible and that all stakeholders are aligned with the plan.

Overseeing Implementation

During the implementation phase, the Solutions Architect provides guidance and oversight to ensure that the solution is built according to the design. This involves working closely with developers, testers, and IT operations to address any issues that arise, making adjustments as necessary to keep the project on track. The Solutions Architect plays a hands-on role in troubleshooting problems, optimising performance, and

221

ensuring that the solution meets both technical and business requirements.

Ensuring Quality and Compliance

The Solutions Architect is responsible for ensuring that the solution meets quality standards and complies with industry regulations and organisational policies. This involves conducting reviews and audits throughout the development process, testing the solution to identify and resolve any issues, and ensuring that security and compliance requirements are met. The Solutions Architect must also ensure that the solution is documented thoroughly to support future maintenance and upgrades.

Continuous Improvement

After the solution is implemented, the Solutions Architect continues to monitor its performance and gather feedback from users and stakeholders. This ongoing evaluation allows the Solutions Architect to identify areas for improvement and make recommendations for future enhancements. The Solutions Architect also stays informed about new technologies and industry trends, ensuring that the organisation's solutions remain competitive and effective over time.

Best Practices for Success as a Solutions Architect

To be successful as a Solutions Architect, certain best practices should be followed:

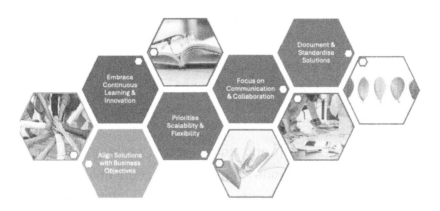

Figure 31: Best Practices for Success as a Solutions Architect

Align Solutions with Business Strategy

Always ensure that the solutions you design are closely aligned with the organisation's strategic goals. This alignment is critical for demonstrating the value of technology investments and ensuring that solutions contribute to the organisation's long-term success.

Prioritise Scalability and Flexibility

Design solutions that are scalable and adaptable to change. The ability to pivot and respond quickly to new business requirements, technological advancements, or market changes is essential for maintaining the relevance and effectiveness of the solution.

Embrace Continuous Learning and Innovation

The technology landscape is constantly evolving, and successful Solutions Architects are those who commit to continuous learning. Stay current with the latest trends, tools, and methodologies in software and system design, and be open to adopting new technologies that can improve the quality and efficiency of your solutions.

Focus on Communication and Collaboration

Strong communication and collaboration skills are essential for success as a Solutions Architect. Foster an environment of open communication, where ideas can be shared freely, and feedback is encouraged. Collaborate with business units, IT teams, and external vendors to ensure that everyone is working towards common goals.

Document and Standardise Solutions

Thorough documentation and standardisation are critical for the success and maintainability of solutions. Ensure that all aspects of the solution, including design decisions, technical specifications, and implementation processes, are well-documented. This practice supports future maintenance and enables other teams to understand and work with the solution effectively.

Learning Exercises to Develop Solutions Architecture Skills

To develop and refine the skills necessary for success as a Solutions Architect, consider the following learning exercises:

Case Study Analysis

Analyse case studies of successful and unsuccessful solution implementations. Identify the key factors that contributed to their outcomes, and reflect on how you would approach similar challenges. This exercise will help you develop critical thinking and problem-solving skills.

Architecture Design Workshops

Participate in or lead workshops focused on system architecture design. Practice creating high-level architecture diagrams, selecting appropriate technologies, and defining system components and interactions. This exercise will help you develop a deeper understanding of system design and improve your ability to create robust and scalable solutions.

Technical Roadmap Development

Practice developing technical roadmaps for hypothetical projects. This exercise will help you improve your ability to plan and manage the implementation of solutions, ensuring that projects are delivered on time and within budget.

Collaboration and Communication Exercises

Engage in exercises that focus on improving communication and collaboration skills. This could involve role-playing scenarios where you must present a technical solution to non-technical stakeholders or work with cross-functional teams to solve a complex problem.

Technology Research and Prototyping

Conduct research on emerging technologies and practice building prototypes using new tools and frameworks. This exercise will help you stay informed about the latest trends and improve your technical proficiency, enabling you to design innovative solutions that leverage cutting-edge technology.

The Application Architect

The Application Architect plays a pivotal role in designing and managing the architecture of software applications within an organisation. Their primary responsibility is to ensure that applications are well-structured, scalable, and aligned with the overall business and IT strategy. Application Architects are tasked with making critical decisions on the frameworks, technologies, and methodologies used to develop software solutions that meet both current and future business needs.

Skills Necessary for an Application Architect

To excel as an Application Architect, a combination of deep technical knowledge, design expertise, and strong interpersonal skills is essential. The following are key skills required for the role:

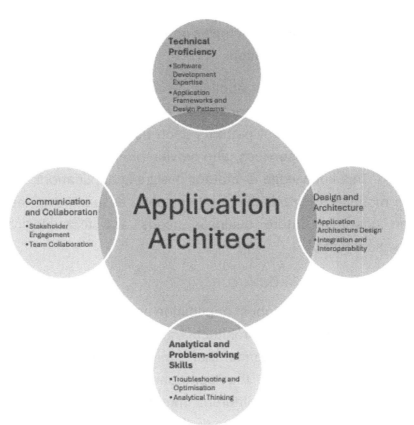

Figure 32: Skills Necessary for an Application Architect

Technical Proficiency

A strong background in software development is essential for an Application Architect. They must be proficient in multiple programming languages such as Go Lang, Java, C#, Python, or JavaScript and have experience with different development frameworks and environments. This technical expertise is critical as it allows the Application Architect to make informed decisions about the technologies and tools that will best meet the needs of the application.

Additionally, mastery of application frameworks and design patterns is crucial. The Application Architect should be well-versed in architectural patterns such as MVC (Model-View-Controller), microservices, and service-oriented architecture (SOA). This knowledge is vital for designing applications that are modular, maintainable, and scalable, ensuring that they can adapt to future business needs and technological advancements.

Design and Architecture

The ability to design robust application architectures is a core skill for an Application Architect. This involves creating high-level architecture blueprints that outline the structure of the application, including the components, data flow, and interactions between different modules. The Application Architect must ensure that the architecture is scalable, flexible, and aligned with the organisation's overall IT strategy. A well-designed architecture supports the long-term success of the application by facilitating easy maintenance and upgrades.

Additionally, ensuring that applications can integrate smoothly with other systems and platforms is critical. The Application Architect must design architectures that support interoperability, allowing the application to communicate effectively with other software systems, databases, and external services. This integration capability is essential for creating cohesive IT environments where all systems work together seamlessly.

Problem-Solving and Analytical Skills

Application Architects must have strong problem-solving skills to diagnose and resolve issues that arise during the development and deployment of applications. This includes identifying performance bottlenecks, addressing security vulnerabilities, and optimising the application for better performance and scalability. Effective problem-solving ensures that the application functions smoothly and meets user expectations.

Additionally, the ability to think analytically is crucial for evaluating different design options and making decisions that balance technical requirements with business objectives. Application Architects must assess the feasibility of proposed solutions and choose the approach that offers the best combination of efficiency, cost-effectiveness, and future-proofing. Analytical thinking enables the architect to anticipate potential challenges and design solutions that are robust and sustainable.

Communication and Collaboration

Effective communication with stakeholders, including business leaders, project managers, developers, and end-users, is essential for an Application Architect. They must be able to translate complex technical concepts into language that non-technical stakeholders can understand, ensuring that everyone is aligned with the project's goals. Clear communication is key to securing buy-in and facilitating smooth project execution.

Additionally, Application Architects often work closely with cross-functional teams, including developers, testers, and IT operations. Strong collaboration skills are necessary to ensure that all team members are working towards a common goal and that the application is delivered on time and within budget. By fostering collaboration and maintaining open lines of communication, the Application Architect helps to ensure the successful development and deployment of the application.

How an Application Architect Performs Their Job

The Application Architect's role involves a wide range of activities, from designing application structures to overseeing their implementation. Here's how an Application Architect typically performs their job:

Figure 33: Typical Application Architect job flow

Understanding Business Requirements

The first step for an Application Architect is to engage with stakeholders to understand the business requirements. This involves conducting meetings and workshops to gather information about the organisation's needs, challenges, and goals. The Application Architect must be able to translate these business requirements into technical specifications that guide the design of the application.

233

Designing the Application Architecture

Based on the gathered requirements, the Application Architect designs the overall architecture of the application. This involves creating high-level architecture diagrams that define the structure of the application, including the components, data flow, and interactions between different modules. The Application Architect must ensure that the architecture is scalable, secure, and maintainable, considering both current and future needs.

Selecting Technologies and Tools

Once the application architecture is designed, the Application Architect selects the appropriate technologies, frameworks, and tools for development. This includes choosing programming languages, development frameworks, databases, and third-party services that align with the application's requirements and the organisation's technology stack.

Overseeing Development and Implementation

During the development phase, the Application Architect provides guidance and oversight to ensure that the application is built according to the design. This involves working closely with developers, testers, and IT operations to address any issues that arise, making adjustments as necessary to keep the project on track. The Application Architect plays a hands-on role in troubleshooting problems, optimising performance, and ensuring that the application meets both technical and business requirements.

Ensuring Quality and Compliance

The Application Architect is responsible for ensuring that the application meets quality standards and complies with industry regulations and organisational policies. This involves conducting code reviews, performance testing, and security assessments to identify and resolve any issues. The Application Architect must also ensure that the application is thoroughly documented to support future maintenance and upgrades.

Continuous Improvement

After the application is deployed, the Application Architect continues to monitor its performance and gather feedback from users and stakeholders. This ongoing evaluation allows the Application Architect to identify areas for improvement and make recommendations for future enhancements. The Application Architect also stays informed about new technologies and industry trends, ensuring that the organisation's applications remain competitive and effective over time.

Best Practices for Success as an Application Architect

To be successful as an Application Architect, certain best practices should be followed:

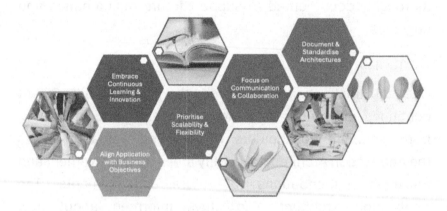

Figure 34: Best Practices for Success as an Application Architect

Align Applications with Business Strategy

Always ensure that the applications you design are closely aligned with the organisation's strategic goals. This alignment is critical for demonstrating the value of technology investments and ensuring that applications contribute to the organisation's long-term success.

Prioritise Scalability and Flexibility

Design application architectures that are scalable and adaptable to change. The ability to pivot and respond quickly to new business requirements, technological advancements, or market changes is essential for maintaining the relevance and effectiveness of the application.

Embrace Continuous Learning and Innovation

The technology landscape is constantly evolving, and successful Application Architects are those who commit to continuous learning. Stay current with the latest trends, tools, and methodologies in software development and architecture, and be open to adopting new technologies that can improve the quality and efficiency of your applications.

Focus on Communication and Collaboration

Strong communication and collaboration skills are essential for success as an Application Architect. Foster an environment of open communication, where ideas can be shared freely, and feedback is encouraged. Collaborate with business units, IT teams, and external vendors to ensure that everyone is working towards common goals.

Document and Standardise Application Architectures

Thorough documentation and standardisation are critical for the success and maintainability of applications. Ensure that all aspects of the application, including design decisions, technical specifications, and development processes, are well-documented. This practice supports future maintenance and enables other teams to understand and work with the application effectively.

Learning Exercises to Develop Application Architecture Skills

To develop and refine the skills necessary for success as an Application Architect, consider the following learning exercises:

Architecture Design Workshops

Participate in or lead workshops focused on application architecture design. Practice creating high-level architecture diagrams, selecting appropriate technologies, and defining system components and interactions. This exercise will help you develop a deeper understanding of system design and improve your ability to create robust and scalable applications.

Code Review and Refactoring Exercises

Engage in code review and refactoring exercises to improve your understanding of best practices in software development. This exercise will help you identify common coding issues, optimise performance, and enhance the maintainability of applications.

Technology Research and Prototyping

Conduct research on emerging technologies and practice building prototypes using new tools and frameworks. This exercise will help you stay informed about the latest trends and improve your technical proficiency, enabling you to design innovative applications that leverage cutting-edge technology.

Collaboration and Communication Exercises

Engage in exercises that focus on improving communication and collaboration skills. This could involve role-playing scenarios where you must present an application architecture to non-technical stakeholders or work with cross-functional teams to solve a complex problem.

Case Study Analysis

Analyse case studies of successful and unsuccessful application implementations. Identify the key factors that contributed to their outcomes, and reflect on how you would approach similar challenges. This exercise will help you develop critical thinking and problem-solving skills.

Architectural Thinking

One of the core skills any architecture must possess is the ability to use "Architectural Thinking". Architectural Thinking is a fundamental approach in both business and technology that involves understanding and solving problems at a higher level of abstraction. Unlike traditional engineering, which often focuses on specific technical implementations, Architectural Thinking encompasses a broader perspective that integrates business goals, technology strategies, and systemic understanding. This approach emphasises solving problems with varying levels of complexity, maintaining a focus on systems as a whole, and utilising modelling to clarify abstract concepts and relationships. It combines insights and heuristics to guide decision-making in complex environments.

Architect vs. Engineer: A Distinct Perspective

The roles of an architect and an engineer are distinct yet complementary. An **architect** focuses on high-level design, strategy, and the alignment of technology with business objectives. Architects look at the bigger picture—how different systems and components fit together to achieve a cohesive whole. They are concerned with frameworks, blueprints, and guidelines that ensure scalability, flexibility, and alignment with strategic goals.

241

On the other hand, an **engineer** is concerned with the detailed implementation and construction of these designs. Engineers deal with the specifics—coding, network configurations, database schemas, and other technical components. While architects create the vision and structure, engineers are the builders who bring that vision to life. In essence, while an architect decides *what* needs to be done and *how* it should be structured, an engineer determines *how* it will be technically executed.

Solving Problems at Different Levels of Complexity

Architectural Thinking requires solving problems at various levels of complexity, ranging from high-level strategic issues to more detailed technical challenges. The ability to navigate and address these different levels of complexity is a key skill for architects, as it allows them to ensure alignment between business goals, IT systems, and operational processes. This section expands on the concept of solving problems at different levels of complexity, providing concrete examples to illustrate how architects approach these challenges.

High-Level Strategic Complexity

At the highest level, architects deal with **strategic complexity**, which involves understanding and aligning business objectives with technological capabilities. This level requires a broad perspective, taking into account multiple stakeholders, diverse business units, and long-term goals. The problems at this level are often ambiguous and require architects to balance competing priorities, such as cost, scalability, and innovation.

Example: Digital Transformation Strategy

Consider a large retail organisation embarking on a **digital transformation** journey. The goal is to enhance customer experience, improve supply chain efficiency, and leverage data analytics for better decision-making. At this level of complexity, the problem is not about choosing a specific technology but rather defining a strategic roadmap that aligns with the company's long-term vision. The architect must evaluate the current IT landscape, identify gaps, and propose a multi-year transformation plan that involves migrating to cloud platforms, integrating e-commerce solutions, and implementing advanced analytics.

In this scenario, the architect must consider factors such as how to prioritise initiatives (e.g., customer-facing applications vs. backend systems), manage change within the organisation, and ensure that the transformation aligns with evolving market trends and customer expectations. They must also plan for future scalability and flexibility, enabling the company to adapt to new technologies and business models.

Intermediate-Level Architectural Complexity

At an intermediate level, architects face **architectural complexity**, where the focus is on designing and integrating systems to meet specific business and technical requirements. This level involves more concrete decision making, such as selecting the right architecture patterns, defining integration points, and ensuring interoperability between different systems.

Example: Building a Microservices-Based Platform

Suppose an organisation decides to modernise its monolithic application into a **microservices-based platform** to achieve better scalability and agility. At this level, the problem is more about architectural design and implementation. The architect must decide on the granularity of microservices, choose a communication protocol (such as REST or gRPC), and ensure proper data consistency across services.

For example, the architect must solve the challenge of managing data consistency In a distributed system. They might choose an eventual consistency model using message queues or event sourcing to ensure that all microservices are synchronised without tightly coupling them. Additionally, the architect needs to implement proper API management and security practices to protect data while ensuring seamless integration with existing systems. The focus here is on creating a scalable, resilient architecture that supports continuous delivery and deployment.

Low-Level Technical Complexity

At the lowest level, architects and engineers face **technical complexity**, which involves specific, detailed challenges related to implementation, performance optimisation, and troubleshooting. While these problems are narrower in scope, they are crucial for ensuring that the solution meets all technical requirements and performs optimally.

Example: Optimising Database Performance in a High-Load Application

Imagine an e-commerce platform experiencing **performance bottlenecks** due to a high volume of concurrent transactions. At this technical level, the problem is to optimise database performance to handle peak loads without degrading user experience. The architect or engineer might need to dive deep into specific technical solutions, such as optimising SQL queries, indexing strategies, or database sharding.

For instance, the architect may implement **database sharding** to distribute data across multiple servers, reducing the load on any single database instance. They might also employ caching mechanisms (e.g., Redis or Memcached) to reduce the number of read operations hitting the database. These technical decisions are focused on solving very specific problems that impact the overall performance of the application.

Cross-Level Problem-Solving: Bridging Strategic and Technical Domains

Architects must often bridge the gap between strategic and technical problem-solving, ensuring that decisions made at different levels are cohesive and aligned. This cross-level problem-solving is critical for maintaining a clear line of sight from business strategy to technical implementation.

Example: Implementing a Hybrid Cloud Strategy

Consider an organisation that decides to adopt a **hybrid cloud strategy** to balance cost, flexibility, and security. At the strategic level, the architect must determine which workloads are best suited for public cloud versus private cloud, considering factors like data sensitivity, regulatory compliance, and cost efficiency. They must create a governance model that ensures data security, manages cloud costs, and provides a framework for multi-cloud management.

At the architectural level, the architect must design a hybrid cloud architecture that seamlessly integrates on-premises systems with cloud environments. This involves selecting the right cloud providers, designing secure VPN connections or direct connectivity (e.g., AWS Direct Connect, Azure ExpressRoute), and implementing hybrid identity and access management.

At the technical level, the architect and engineering teams must ensure that the network configuration, data replication mechanisms, and monitoring tools are properly set up to support a hybrid cloud model. They need to implement specific solutions like **container orchestration** (e.g., Kubernetes) that allow applications to run consistently across both cloud and on-premises environments.

Addressing Multi-Dimensional Problems: The Systems Approach

Architectural Thinking involves addressing problems that span multiple dimensions—technical, organisational, operational, and strategic. The **systems approach** ensures that all these dimensions are considered and integrated into a cohesive solution.

Example: Developing a Smart City Infrastructure

Designing a **smart city infrastructure** involves multi-dimensional problem-solving. At the strategic level, the goal is to create a sustainable and efficient urban environment that improves the quality of life for citizens. This involves integrating various domains, such as transportation, energy, public safety, and healthcare.

At the architectural level, the architect must design a system that integrates various IoT sensors, data analytics platforms, and communication networks. This requires decisions about data interoperability standards, cybersecurity measures, and data privacy policies.

At the technical level, specific challenges might include ensuring low-latency communication between IoT devices, optimising data storage and processing capabilities, and implementing machine learning models to analyse real-time data.

Architectural Thinking involves solving problems at different levels of complexity, from high-level strategic decisions to detailed technical implementations. It requires a systems approach that considers all aspects of a problem, ensuring that solutions are comprehensive and cohesive. By mastering the ability to navigate and address these various levels of complexity, architects can create architectures that align with business goals, leverage technology effectively, and drive organisational success. The examples shared above (digital transformation strategies, microservices-based platforms, database optimisations, hybrid cloud strategies, and smart city infrastructures) illustrates the wide range of challenges that architects face and the skills required to address them.

A Systems Approach: Focusing on Systems as a Whole

Architectural Thinking adopts a **systems approach**, focusing on systems as a whole rather than isolated components. This perspective recognises that an organisation's IT landscape is made up of interconnected systems that work together to deliver value. An architectural thinker considers not only the individual parts but also the relationships and interactions between these parts.

The **systems approach** to architecture is a holistic way of thinking that focuses on understanding and managing complex, interrelated systems as a whole rather than in isolated parts. This approach considers all the components of a system—including people, processes, technology, and data—as interconnected entities that must work together to achieve common goals. It emphasises the interactions between these components, the emergent properties that arise from these interactions, and the optimisation of the system as a whole.

In the context of Enterprise Architecture, the systems approach helps architects design, manage, and optimise the overall architecture of an organisation to ensure alignment with business objectives, operational efficiency, and flexibility to adapt to future changes.

Key Principles of the Systems Approach

Holistic View

Consider the organisation as an integrated whole, where various systems, processes, and technologies are interdependent.

Interconnected Components

Focus on how different parts of the system interact with each other, rather than treating them as isolated entities.

Emergent Properties

Recognise that the behaviour of the entire system cannot always be predicted by understanding individual components; new behaviours emerge from the interaction of these parts.

Feedback Loops

Monitor how changes in one part of the system affect others, and use feedback to make continuous improvements.

Alignment with Purpose

Ensure that every component and interaction aligns with the organisation's strategic objectives.

Examples of the Systems Approach in Practice

The systems approach is applied in various architectural scenarios to ensure coherence, adaptability, and resilience. Here are some concrete examples:

Smart City Infrastructure Development

A **smart city** integrates multiple domains like transportation, energy, healthcare, public safety, and utilities into a cohesive urban system. The systems approach is essential in designing a smart city infrastructure that functions efficiently and sustainably.

Holistic View	The architect considers the entire city as a single, interconnected system. Transportation networks, energy grids, public safety, and communication systems must all be integrated to provide a seamless urban experience.
Interconnected Components	The smart city system includes IoT sensors, cloud platforms, data analytics, and machine learning algorithms that work together to manage traffic flow, energy consumption, waste management, and emergency services.

Emergent Properties	By integrating these domains, new capabilities such as predictive traffic management and automated energy distribution emerge, which are not possible when each system operates independently.
Feedback Loops	Real-time data from sensors (e.g., traffic cameras, air quality monitors) is analysed to make adjustments, such as rerouting traffic or increasing energy supply during peak hours.
Alignment with Purpose	The purpose is to enhance the quality of life for citizens by creating an efficient, safe, and sustainable urban environment. All subsystems must align with this purpose, from public transport to healthcare delivery systems.

Hybrid Cloud Strategy Implementation

In a **hybrid cloud strategy**, an organisation uses a mix of on-premises, private cloud, and public cloud services to achieve the optimal balance of cost, flexibility, and security. A systems approach is vital to ensure that all these environments work together seamlessly.

Holistic View	The architect views the IT environment as a unified system that must seamlessly integrate on-premises data centres with public cloud environments like AWS, Azure, or Google Cloud.
Interconnected Components	Components such as network connectivity (VPNs, Direct Connect), identity management

	(e.g., Azure AD, AWS IAM), and data synchronisation (e.g., hybrid databases, cloud storage) must be tightly integrated to ensure a seamless user experience.
Emergent Properties	The hybrid cloud architecture allows the organisation to achieve both scalability and control. For example, sensitive data can remain on-premises while leveraging the cloud for scaling computational workloads
Feedback Loops	Continuous monitoring and feedback are critical for managing costs, optimising performance, and maintaining security. For instance, a sudden spike in cloud costs could trigger a policy review to identify inefficiencies.
Alignment with Purpose	The goal is to leverage the cloud's scalability and flexibility while maintaining control and compliance over critical data. All integration points and processes are designed to support this hybrid cloud strategy.

Enterprise Resource Planning (ERP) System Integration

Integrating an **ERP system** within an organisation's existing IT ecosystem involves multiple business functions, such as finance, HR, procurement, and supply chain. The systems approach ensures that the ERP system seamlessly integrates and interacts with existing systems to provide a unified and efficient operation.

Holistic View	The architect views the organisation as a system where data flows between ERP modules (finance, HR) and other systems (CRM, supply chain management).
Interconnected Components	Integration points such as APIs, data pipelines, and middleware are designed to enable seamless communication and data exchange between the ERP and other systems.
Emergent Properties	With seamless integration, new capabilities such as real-time financial reporting or automated inventory replenishment emerge, which enhance decision-making and operational efficiency.
Feedback Loops	The ERP system continually gathers data from various departments, providing feedback to improve processes like demand forecasting or workforce planning.
Alignment with Purpose	The ERP system's purpose is to streamline operations and provide a single source of truth for organisational data. All integrations and process flows are designed to serve this overarching goal.

Customer 360 Strategy in a Financial Institution

A **Customer 360 strategy** aims to provide a unified view of customers across multiple channels and touchpoints, allowing organisations to deliver personalised and consistent experiences. A systems approach is crucial to integrate data from various customer-facing systems.

Holistic View	The architect considers all customer touchpoints (web, mobile, call centres, branches) as parts of a single system aimed at understanding customer behaviour and delivering a personalised experience.
Interconnected Components	Data integration tools (ETL processes, data lakes), customer relationship management (CRM) systems, and analytics platforms are interconnected to enable a unified view of the customer.
Emergent Properties	By integrating these components, the organisation can provide tailored financial products and services, predictive analytics for customer retention, and enhanced fraud detection capabilities.
Feedback Loops	Continuous feedback from customer interactions is analysed to improve services, refine marketing strategies, and enhance customer satisfaction.
Alignment with Purpose	The ultimate purpose is to increase customer loyalty and lifetime value by providing personalised, data-driven experiences. All systems and processes are integrated to serve this goal.

Healthcare Ecosystem Integration

Integrating a **healthcare ecosystem** involves multiple entities, such as hospitals, pharmacies, insurance companies, and government bodies. A systems approach ensures that patient data, healthcare services, and billing systems work together seamlessly to provide high-quality care.

Holistic View	The architect views the healthcare ecosystem as a unified system that must coordinate care delivery, manage patient data, and ensure compliance with regulations.
Interconnected Components	Integration points such as electronic health records (EHRs), health information exchanges (HIEs), and interoperability standards (HL7, FHIR) are essential to enable seamless communication between different healthcare providers.
Emergent Properties	Integrated healthcare ecosystems enable new capabilities, such as coordinated care management and real-time patient monitoring, which can significantly improve patient outcomes.
Feedback Loops	Patient data and treatment outcomes provide feedback that informs policy changes, improves care guidelines, and enhances clinical decision-making.
Alignment with Purpose	The purpose is to provide holistic, patient-centred care while reducing costs and improving outcomes. All integration efforts and data flows are aligned with these objectives.

The systems approach to architecture is a comprehensive method that ensures all components of a system are designed, integrated, and managed cohesively to achieve the organisation's goals. By focusing on the system as a whole, understanding the interactions between components, leveraging feedback loops, and aligning with the purpose, architects can create robust and flexible architectures that drive business success.

Purpose: The Core of Architectural Thinking

Understanding the **purpose** of a system or solution is central to the systems approach in architectural thinking. Purpose defines why a system exists and drives all architectural decisions. It is the foundation upon which architects build and design their solutions, ensuring that every component, interaction, and process aligns with the organisation's overarching goals. Without a clear understanding of purpose, an architectural approach may lack direction, coherence, and effectiveness.

The concept of purpose extends beyond just solving immediate problems; it involves understanding the organisation's long-term vision and mission and aligning the architecture to support these broader objectives. Purpose provides clarity in decision-making, ensuring that all design and implementation choices contribute to the intended outcomes and add value to the organisation.

Key Aspects of Purpose in Architectural Thinking

Alignment with Business Strategy

Every architectural decision should support the organisation's strategic goals. Whether the goal is to improve customer experience, increase operational efficiency, or enable digital transformation, the architecture must be designed to facilitate these outcomes. For example, in a retail organisation focused on improving customer engagement through digital channels, the purpose of the architecture might be to provide a seamless omnichannel experience. This would drive decisions around integrating CRM, e-commerce platforms, mobile apps, and analytics tools to create a cohesive customer journey.

Guiding Design and Integration Choices

Purpose serves as a guiding principle when making design and integration choices. Architects need to decide on architecture patterns, integration strategies, and technology stacks that best fulfil the system's intended purpose. For instance, a healthcare system focused on patient-centred care would prioritise interoperability and data security to ensure that different healthcare providers can securely share patient data. This purpose would guide the architect to choose standards like HL7 and FHIR for interoperability and robust encryption methods for data security.

Driving Innovation and Adaptability

When purpose is clearly defined, it allows the architecture to adapt and innovate over time. An architecture that is purpose-driven is not static; it evolves to meet changing business needs and technological advancements. For example, a financial institution aiming to become a leader in digital banking will have an architecture purpose-built for agility, scalability, and innovation. This might involve adopting a microservices architecture that allows for rapid development and deployment of new features, enabling the institution to quickly respond to market demands.

Ensuring Consistency Across Systems

A well-defined purpose helps ensure consistency across different systems and components. When all parts of the architecture are aligned with a common purpose, it prevents fragmentation and siloed development. In a smart city initiative, the purpose could be to create an efficient and sustainable urban environment. This would ensure that all subsystems— such as transportation, energy, waste management, and public safety—are designed to work together seamlessly, rather than being developed in isolation.

Facilitating Stakeholder Communication and Buy-In

Clearly articulating the purpose of an architecture helps in gaining stakeholder buy-in. When stakeholders understand how the architecture will help achieve strategic objectives, they are more likely to support the necessary investments and changes. For example, in an organisation planning to implement a hybrid cloud strategy, explaining that the purpose is to balance flexibility with control can help align IT teams, business leaders, and compliance officers on the need for such an approach.

Providing a Framework for Measuring Success

Purpose also provides a framework for evaluating the success of an architectural initiative. By defining what success looks like in terms of business outcomes (such as increased revenue, improved customer satisfaction, or reduced operational costs), architects can set metrics and KPIs to measure the effectiveness of their solutions. For instance, if the purpose of a new ERP system is to streamline operations and reduce costs, success can be measured by tracking reductions in process cycle times, error rates, and cost savings.

Examples of Purpose-Driven Architecture

To better understand how purpose drives architectural thinking, consider the following real-world examples:

E-Commerce Platform for Rapid Growth

Purpose	An e-commerce company aims to become the leading online retailer in its region by providing a fast, reliable, and personalised shopping experience.
Architectural Decisions	The purpose guides the architect to choose a scalable cloud-based architecture that can handle peak traffic during sales and promotions. Microservices are adopted to allow for rapid development and deployment of new features, while data analytics tools are integrated to provide personalised product recommendations.

Outcome	The architecture supports the company's purpose by enabling fast page loads, smooth checkout experiences, and personalised marketing, driving customer satisfaction and repeat business.

Public Sector Data Sharing Initiative

Purpose	A government initiative seeks to improve data sharing across various public sector departments to enhance decision-making and service delivery.
Architectural Decisions	The purpose drives the need for a centralised data platform that integrates data from health, education, transportation, and public safety departments. The architecture emphasises data governance, interoperability standards, and secure APIs to ensure data privacy and regulatory compliance.
Outcome	The purpose-driven architecture enables better resource allocation, more informed policy-making, and improved citizen services by providing a unified view of public sector data.

Banking Platform for Financial Inclusion

Purpose	A financial institution wants to expand its services to underbanked communities, providing accessible and affordable banking solutions.
Architectural Decisions	The architecture is designed to be lightweight and mobile-first, as many users may only have access to smartphones. It focuses on integrating digital wallets, low-cost payment gateways, and simplified account management systems. Security is also a priority, with multi-factor authentication and fraud detection systems built into the core architecture.
Outcome	By aligning with the purpose of financial inclusion, the architecture supports the development of an easy-to-use, secure mobile banking app that reaches underserved communities, increasing the institution's market presence and customer base.

The concept of **purpose** is a cornerstone of the systems approach to architecture. It acts as a compass that guides all architectural decisions, ensuring that they are aligned with strategic objectives, business goals, and desired outcomes. Whether the purpose is to enhance customer experience, streamline operations, promote sustainability, or drive innovation, it must be clearly defined and consistently applied throughout the architecture. By focusing on purpose, architects can create cohesive, adaptable, and effective solutions that deliver maximum value to the organisation and its stakeholders.

How Modelling Helps in Architectural Thinking

Modelling is an essential tool in architectural thinking, providing a visual and abstract representation of complex systems, processes, and relationships. It helps architects and stakeholders understand, analyse, and communicate the design and structure of a solution or system. Modelling allows for a simplified view of reality, enabling better decision-making, risk management, and strategic planning. By creating models, architects can explore different scenarios, validate assumptions, identify potential issues, and ensure alignment with business goals and technical requirements.

Key Benefits of Modelling in Architecture

Clarification of Complex Systems

Modelling helps break down complex systems into understandable components, making it easier to analyse and comprehend their interactions. In large organisations with interconnected IT systems, business processes, and data flows, models provide a clear visual map that shows how different parts work together. This clarity is crucial for identifying dependencies, potential bottlenecks, and areas for optimisation.

Example: In designing an enterprise data architecture, a model can illustrate how data flows from source systems (like ERP and CRM) to a data warehouse and then to analytics platforms. This helps in understanding how data is collected, processed, and consumed, making it easier to identify any inefficiencies or gaps.

Facilitating Communication and Collaboration

Models serve as a common language between various stakeholders—such as business leaders, developers, IT teams, and external partners. By providing a visual representation, models help bridge the gap between technical and non-technical stakeholders, ensuring that everyone has a shared understanding of the architecture and its objectives. This is critical for gaining buy-in, aligning expectations, and facilitating effective collaboration.

Example: A model of a customer journey map, showing all touchpoints and interactions with an organisation's digital platforms, can be used to communicate with both marketing teams (to optimise customer experience) and IT teams (to ensure seamless integration of systems).

Enabling Better Decision-Making and Scenario Analysis:

Modelling allows architects to simulate different scenarios and analyse their impact before actual implementation. This is particularly valuable for decision-making, as it enables the evaluation of various options based on feasibility, cost, performance, and risk. By exploring multiple scenarios, architects can choose the most effective solution that aligns with business goals.

> **Example**: When planning a cloud migration strategy, models can help visualise different cloud architectures (hybrid, multi-cloud, private) and assess the trade-offs in terms of cost, security, and scalability. This helps the organisation decide on the best approach.

Improving Risk Management and Mitigation

Models help in identifying potential risks and dependencies early in the design phase. By visualising the architecture, architects can pinpoint where vulnerabilities may exist, such as single points of failure, data bottlenecks, or security gaps. This allows for proactive risk mitigation, reducing the likelihood of costly rework or system failures later in the project lifecycle.

Example: In cybersecurity architecture, modelling the data flow between various systems helps identify critical points where encryption, firewalls, and intrusion detection systems need to be implemented. This foresight can prevent potential breaches and protect sensitive data.

Supporting Documentation and Standardisation

Models provide a structured and standardised way to document the architecture, which is essential for future reference, maintenance, and governance. A well-documented model ensures consistency in understanding and implementation, reducing the risk of misinterpretation or misalignment during execution. Standardisation through modelling also helps in maintaining architectural consistency across different projects and teams.

Example: A model using UML (Unified Modelling Language) can standardise the documentation of a software application's architecture, including class diagrams, sequence diagrams, and deployment diagrams. This helps developers and engineers to follow the same conventions and understand the system's design.

Driving Alignment with Business Goals

Modelling ensures that the architecture aligns with business goals by providing a clear link between technical design and business objectives. It helps in visualising how different architectural components contribute to achieving business outcomes, such as increasing revenue, improving customer satisfaction, or enhancing operational efficiency.

Example: In an insurance company, modelling the end-to-end claims processing workflow can help ensure that IT systems are designed to reduce processing time, minimise manual errors, and enhance customer experience, directly supporting business goals.

Facilitating Agile and Iterative Development:

In agile environments, models provide a flexible and iterative way to design and evolve architectures. Architects can use models to quickly test new ideas, validate assumptions, and make adjustments as needed without committing to costly changes. This iterative modelling approach supports continuous improvement and adaptation to changing requirements.

Example: In developing a microservices architecture, models can represent service interactions and dependencies. As new services are added or modified, models are updated to reflect the changes, ensuring that the architecture remains aligned with the overall business strategy.

Types of Models Used in Architectural Thinking

Conceptual Models

These models provide a high-level view of the system, focusing on the relationships between major components and how they align with business objectives. Conceptual models help in understanding the overall architecture without getting into technical details.

> **Example**: A conceptual model of a digital transformation initiative might show how various components—like customer relationship management (CRM), supply chain management (SCM), and data analytics—are interconnected to achieve business goals.
>
>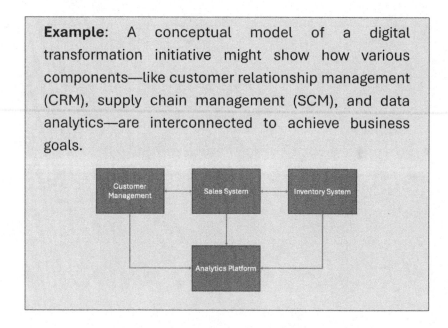

Logical Models

Logical models go a level deeper, detailing the structure and relationships of the system components without specifying the physical implementation. These models help in understanding how data flows through the system, how components interact, and how processes are managed.

Example: A logical model for an e-commerce platform might detail how different microservices (user authentication, product catalogue, payment gateway) interact and exchange data to fulfil a customer order.

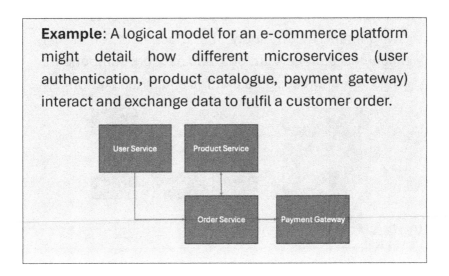

Physical Models

Physical models represent the actual implementation of the system, including hardware, network configurations, database schemas, and software components. These models are essential for the detailed design and deployment phases.

Example: A physical model for a hybrid cloud environment might show the placement of virtual machines, storage solutions, and network components across on-premises data centres and cloud platforms.

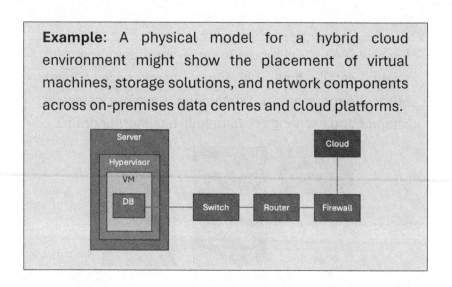

Process Models

Process models describe how business processes flow within the system, including the sequence of activities, decision points, and interactions between various roles and systems. These models are crucial for optimising business workflows and ensuring system alignment with business processes.

Example: A process model for loan approval in a bank would illustrate each step, from application submission to credit assessment, approval, and disbursement, showing the interaction between different departments and IT systems.

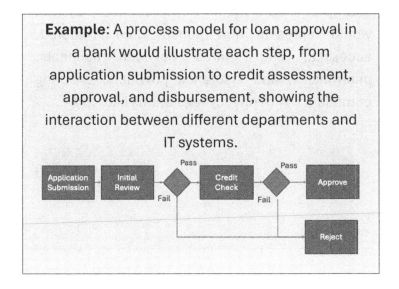

Data Models

Data models focus on how data is structured, stored, and accessed within a system. They help in designing databases, ensuring data integrity, and optimising data flow across different components.

> **Example:** A data model for a healthcare system would represent how patient data is stored, accessed, and shared between hospitals, pharmacies, and insurance providers, ensuring compliance with privacy regulations like HIPAA.
>
>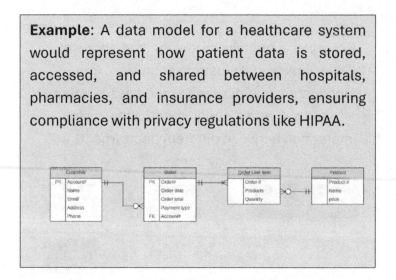

Modelling is an indispensable part of architectural thinking, offering a powerful way to visualise, analyse, and communicate complex systems. By providing clarity, enabling better decision-making, improving risk management, and ensuring alignment with business goals, models help architects design robust, scalable, and adaptable architectures. Different types of models—conceptual, logical, physical, process, and data—serve different purposes, from high-level strategy planning to detailed implementation. Together, these models provide a comprehensive toolkit for architects to navigate complexity and deliver value through well-designed solutions.

Insights vs. Heuristics: A Key Distinction in Architectural Thinking

Architectural thinking relies heavily on both **insights** and **heuristics** to guide decision-making in complex environments. While both are critical tools for architects, they serve different purposes and function in unique ways when navigating architectural challenges. Understanding the distinction between insights and heuristics is essential for effectively applying architectural thinking to design solutions that are robust, adaptable, and aligned with business goals.

What are Insights?

Insights are deep, often novel understandings or realisations about a problem, system, or environment. They are typically derived from in-depth analysis, experience, research, or critical thinking. Insights provide a clear and comprehensive understanding of a particular issue or opportunity, often revealing underlying causes, patterns, or dynamics that were not immediately apparent.

Insights are characterised by their ability to provide clarity and direction. They allow architects to see the "big picture" and understand how different elements of a system interact, enabling more informed and strategic decision-making. Insights are often specific to a particular context and can lead to innovative solutions that are both effective and efficient.

Example of Insight:

In an organisation facing slow decision-making processes due to siloed information systems, an architect might gain an insight that the root cause is not just technical but also cultural—a lack of data sharing and collaboration between departments. This insight could lead to a solution that involves not only integrating IT systems but also fostering a culture of collaboration and transparency, resulting in more effective decision-making.

What are Heuristics?

Heuristics are practical, experience-based techniques or rules of thumb that help architects navigate complexity and make decisions when faced with uncertainty. Unlike insights, which provide deep understanding and specific solutions, heuristics are general guidelines or approaches that offer a way to solve problems based on prior experiences or established best practices.

Heuristics are valuable because they simplify decision-making processes in complex or ambiguous situations. They do not guarantee the "best" solution but often provide a "good enough" solution quickly, which is useful when time, data, or resources are limited. Heuristics are typically more flexible and can be applied across different contexts with some degree of modification.

> **Example of Heuristic:**
>
> A common heuristic in enterprise architecture might be: "Design for scalability first, then optimise for cost later." This heuristic is useful because it provides a general approach for handling growth and capacity concerns. By designing systems that can scale, an architect ensures that the architecture can handle future demands, and only later focuses on cost optimisation once the need for scalability is addressed.

Key Differences Between Insights and Heuristics

Nature and Origin

Insights are often context-specific and arise from deep analysis, experience, and a thorough understanding of a particular situation. They are revelations that offer a new perspective or a deeper understanding of a problem.

Heuristics are general rules of thumb that stem from accumulated experience and knowledge. They are not specific to one situation but can be applied to various contexts, providing a baseline for action.

Purpose and Application

Insights aim to provide clarity and uncover underlying causes or solutions. They help architects understand "why" something is happening and "what" needs to be done.

Heuristics provide practical guidance on "how" to approach a problem. They are particularly useful when an architect needs to make a quick decision or when data and resources are limited.

Certainty and Reliability

Insights are often more reliable because they are based on deep understanding and analysis. However, they may require more time and effort to develop.

Heuristics are quicker to apply but may not always lead to the optimal solution. They are useful in guiding decisions but should be used with an awareness of their limitations.

Flexibility and Adaptability:

Insights are typically less flexible as they are deeply tied to specific contexts and problems. The same insight may not apply universally.

Heuristics are highly adaptable and can be modified or adjusted to fit different situations. Their general nature makes them broadly applicable, though sometimes at the cost of precision.

When to Use Insights vs. Heuristics in Architecture

Use Insights When:

- The problem is complex and requires a deep understanding to be solved effectively.
- There is sufficient time and data to analyse the problem thoroughly.
- A unique or innovative solution is needed that goes beyond standard approaches.
- There is a need to change the strategic direction or rethink fundamental assumptions.

Use Heuristics When:

- Time is limited, and a quick decision is necessary.
- The problem is familiar, and there is past experience to draw from.
- The cost of a suboptimal decision is low, and flexibility is more important than precision.

- The environment is highly dynamic, and decisions need to be adjusted frequently.

Examples of Insights vs. Heuristics in Architectural Practice

Example in Cloud Migration

Insight: After analysing a company's current IT landscape and operational costs, an architect might gain the insight that the primary cost driver is not just the number of servers but the inefficiency of workload distribution across hybrid environments. This insight might lead to a restructuring of workloads, optimising them for cost and performance based on specific business needs.

Heuristic: A heuristic in cloud migration might be, "Start with non-critical workloads to gain experience and build confidence." This heuristic allows the organisation to move to the cloud incrementally, reducing risk and allowing teams to learn and adapt before migrating critical systems.

Example in Security Architecture

Insight: Analysing the flow of sensitive data across various departments, an architect may realise that a significant security risk arises from improper access control and lack of encryption in internal data transfers. This insight would lead to a focused solution on implementing robust access control mechanisms and end-to-end encryption.

Heuristic: A common heuristic in security architecture might be, "Trust but verify—implement multi-factor authentication (MFA) for all critical systems." This provides a quick way to enhance security without needing to fully redesign existing authentication systems.

Example in Microservices Design

Insight: By examining an organisation's monolithic application architecture and its scaling challenges, an architect might gain the insight that the core problem is the tight coupling of unrelated services, which causes bottlenecks. This insight would lead to decomposing the monolith into loosely coupled microservices that can scale independently.

Heuristic: A heuristic for microservices design might be, "Keep services small and focused on a single responsibility." This heuristic helps prevent creating tightly coupled services, even if the architect does not have detailed insights into every potential interaction between services.

Combining Insights and Heuristics for Effective Architectural Thinking

Successful architectural thinking often involves a combination of both insights and heuristics. Insights provide the depth and understanding needed to address complex challenges, while heuristics offer practical guidance that helps navigate ambiguity and make decisions faster. By leveraging both, architects can create well-balanced solutions that are both strategically aligned and practically feasible.

> **Example**: In designing an enterprise integration strategy, an architect might use the insight that a decentralised data architecture would better support the company's agile development needs and prevent bottlenecks. Meanwhile, a heuristic like "Use APIs for integration wherever possible" provides a straightforward rule to ensure flexibility and maintainability without needing deep analysis for every integration point.

Insights and heuristics are complementary tools in architectural thinking, each offering unique advantages. Insights provide a deep, context-specific understanding that leads to innovative and tailored solutions, while heuristics offer practical, experience-based rules that guide decision-making in uncertain or dynamic situations. By understanding and leveraging both, architects can navigate complex challenges, align with strategic goals, and deliver robust, scalable, and effective architectures.

Architectural Thinking is a holistic approach that integrates technical knowledge, business understanding, and systemic insight to design solutions that align with organisational goals. It distinguishes itself from traditional engineering by focusing on higher levels of abstraction, purpose-driven design, and a systems approach. Modelling serves as a critical tool for visualising complex systems, while insights and heuristics provide the guidance needed to navigate challenges and make informed decisions. By mastering these concepts, architects can create robust, scalable, and effective architectures that drive business success.

Art Complements Science
in Architecture

In the realm of architecture—whether it is software, enterprise, or systems architecture—there is an essential interplay between **art and science**. While science provides the foundational principles, methodologies, and structured processes that guide architecture, art brings creativity, intuition, and human experience into play. This combination of art and science is vital for creating innovative, practical, and human-cantered solutions that go beyond conventional thinking.

The Role of Art in Architecting

The **art of architecting** is crucial for envisioning unprecedented and novel applications. While science focuses on measurable, repeatable phenomena, art excels in areas where science is less effective—dealing with ambiguity, interpreting abstract ideas, and applying wisdom gleaned from past experience to new contexts. In essence, art in architecture is about **seeing beyond the obvious**, conceptualising solutions that are not strictly derived from data or formulas but are inspired by a deeper understanding of human needs, emotions, and experiences.

Conceptualisation and Innovation

Art enables architects to conceptualise bold new ideas that may not fit neatly into existing frameworks or scientific models. This is especially important in the early stages of a project when the focus is on exploring possibilities, imagining what

283

could be, and structuring those imaginative concepts into something technically feasible. For instance, designing an innovative customer experience for a digital platform requires more than just technical know-how; it demands an empathetic understanding of user behaviours, needs, and emotions.

Applying Past Experience and Wisdom

Art allows architects to leverage intuition and judgment based on accumulated experience and wisdom. Where scientific methods may fall short in providing clear answers, art complements by enabling architects to draw on their deep, often tacit knowledge to make decisions that are not only technically sound but also strategically wise. This is particularly valuable when working in uncharted territory, such as designing solutions for emerging technologies or rapidly evolving markets.

Sanity Checks and Balancing Ambiguity

In the face of uncertainty, art provides **sanity checks** that help architects avoid being overly reliant on rigid frameworks or data-driven models. It introduces a layer of pragmatism and human insight that ensures solutions are not just theoretically optimal but practically applicable. For example, while science might suggest the most efficient database design, art might dictate a more user-friendly interface that ultimately provides greater business value.

How the Nature of Architecting Changes Across Phases

The **nature of architecting** evolves as a **project progresses** through different phases—from initial ideation and conceptualisation to detailed design and implementation. The balance between art and science shifts throughout these stages, highlighting the need for a flexible and adaptive approach.

Earliest Stages: Structuring Hopes, Needs, and Dreams

In the earliest stages of a project, architecture is more about **structuring hopes, needs, and dreams** into feasible technical possibilities. This is where the art of architecture truly shines. At this phase:

Vision and Imagination

Architects are tasked with translating abstract desires—such as enhancing customer satisfaction, creating a disruptive product, or building a resilient IT infrastructure—into a vision that can be realised through technology. This requires creativity and out-of-the-box thinking to visualise what is possible, not just what is practical.

Synthesising Diverse Inputs

At this stage, the architect must synthesise inputs from various stakeholders, including business leaders, users, and technical teams. This involves understanding and reconciling different perspectives, aspirations, and even emotions. Here, art is used to create a narrative that resonates with all stakeholders, framing technical solutions in a way that aligns with broader organisational goals and human needs.

Navigating Uncertainty

The early stages are marked by uncertainty and ambiguity, where not all variables are known, and the direction may not be entirely clear. Here, the art of architecting involves creating prototypes, experimenting with different models, and embracing a degree of risk to explore innovative approaches that may later become the foundation of the architecture.

Later Stages: Integration and Mediation Among Competing Subsystems

As the project moves into the later stages, the role of the architect shifts to **integration and mediation among competing subsystems and interests**. This phase is more about **balancing technical rigor with human-centred considerations** and ensuring that the architecture remains coherent and aligned with the initial vision.

Normative and Rational Methods

At this point, the scientific aspect of architecture comes to the forefront. The focus is on applying normative methods—established best practices, frameworks, and standards—to ensure that the architecture is robust, scalable, secure, and compliant. Here, science guides the integration of various subsystems, such as ensuring seamless data flow between an ERP system and a CRM platform, or managing API connections in a microservices architecture.

Mediating Conflicting Interests

The art aspect becomes critical again as the architect must mediate between different stakeholders who may have conflicting interests or priorities. For instance, the marketing team may prioritise customer engagement features, while the IT team focuses on security and performance. The architect uses both art (diplomacy, negotiation, empathy) and science (technical feasibility, trade-off analysis) to reconcile these differences and guide the project to a successful outcome.

Adapting to Changing Requirements

Even in the later stages, the need for adaptability remains. While normative methods provide stability, the art of architecture allows for flexibility to adjust to evolving requirements, emerging technologies, or unforeseen challenges. This adaptability ensures that the architecture remains relevant and effective throughout its lifecycle.

The Synergy Between Art and Science in Architecture

The fusion of art and science in architecture creates a powerful approach that balances creativity with precision, fostering innovative yet reliable solutions. Architects who effectively integrate both aspects can deliver systems and structures that not only meet technical requirements but also resonate with human needs, organisational culture, and long-term strategic goals. Let's delve deeper into the three core areas where this balance is most impactful: balancing technical excellence with human-centred design, fostering innovation while ensuring reliability, and creating enduring and adaptive architectures.

Balancing Technical Excellence with Human-Centred Design

Effective architects understand that **technical excellence** alone is not sufficient; solutions must also be **human-centred**. Technical excellence, driven by science, involves creating architectures that are robust, efficient, scalable, and secure. It focuses on optimising systems to perform at their best under varying conditions, utilising data-driven methods, standards, and best practices to achieve reliability and consistency.

However, **human-centred design**—the art aspect—emphasises creating systems that are intuitive, user-friendly, and aligned with the needs and behaviours of the people who interact with them. This means understanding the user's perspective, considering how they engage with technology, and ensuring that the design is inclusive, accessible, and emotionally resonant.

Finding the Right Balance

The challenge for architects is to find the balance between these two aspects. A technically flawless system that is difficult to use or doesn't align with the organisation's culture can lead to low adoption rates, dissatisfaction, or failure to deliver the desired outcomes. Conversely, a system that is beautifully designed for users but lacks technical soundness can lead to performance issues, security vulnerabilities, or scalability problems. Successful architects combine both, ensuring that their designs are not only innovative and technically robust but also practical and user-centred.

Example:

Consider the design of a public transportation app. From a technical standpoint, it needs to handle real-time data, provide accurate scheduling information, and integrate with various payment systems. From a human-centred design perspective, the app must be intuitive, provide clear and simple navigation, accommodate accessibility needs, and offer a seamless user experience. Balancing these two aspects ensures that the app is both technically efficient and meets the diverse needs of its users.

Fostering Innovation While Ensuring Reliability

Innovation in architecture often involves **breaking away from established norms** and experimenting with new possibilities. This artistic side of architecture encourages architects to think creatively, explore unconventional solutions, and push the boundaries of what is possible. Innovation is crucial for staying competitive, adapting to market changes, and addressing new challenges with fresh approaches.

However, innovation must be tempered with **reliability** and **scalability**, which are rooted in scientific principles. Reliability ensures that systems perform consistently under expected and unexpected conditions, while scalability guarantees that the system can grow with the organisation's needs. Science, with its emphasis on proven methodologies, repeatability, and standards, provides the stability that underpins innovation.

Knowing When to Innovate and When to Standardise

The art of architecture lies in knowing when to prioritise innovation and when to adhere to established practices. Architects must assess the risk, cost, and potential benefits of innovative solutions and decide whether to pursue new paths or rely on tried-and-tested methods. For instance, while developing a new product or service, an architect might opt for a cutting-edge microservices architecture to support rapid innovation. In contrast, for a mission-critical system requiring high reliability, they may choose more conventional, monolithic architecture patterns that are well-understood and stable.

Practical Examples

In cloud architecture, adopting a multi-cloud strategy may offer innovative flexibility and resilience but comes with complexity and potential reliability challenges. The architect must carefully evaluate the balance, ensuring that innovation (multi-cloud flexibility) does not undermine reliability (consistency and manageability).

Creating Enduring and Adaptive Architectures

The ultimate goal of architecture is to create systems that are **effective today** and **adaptable for the future**. This requires an understanding that systems must be sustainable, scalable, and capable of evolving as needs and technologies change. **Enduring architectures** are those that are not only built to last but are also designed to adapt and grow over time.

Art and Science in Future-Proofing

The art in architecture involves envisioning future possibilities and designing with flexibility in mind, while the science ensures that the foundation is stable, secure, and compliant with standards. Architects use **artistic foresight** to anticipate changes—whether technological advances, shifts in user needs, or regulatory changes—and plan for them. Simultaneously, they use **scientific principles** to ensure that the architecture remains robust, with strong foundations that can support future modifications.

Building in Adaptability

One practical approach to creating enduring architectures is to use modular and loosely coupled designs. For example, a microservices architecture, where components are independent and can be updated, replaced, or scaled individually, provides flexibility and adaptability. This contrasts with a monolithic architecture that, while simpler initially, may become rigid and costly to modify as requirements evolve.

Practical Examples

Consider a global e-commerce platform that anticipates future expansions into new markets. An enduring architecture would not only handle current traffic and transaction volumes but would also be designed to integrate new payment systems, languages, and compliance requirements. Using both art (envisioning market expansion needs) and science (designing a scalable and modular architecture), architects can create a system that is both adaptable and robust.

The effective integration of **art and science** in architecture results in solutions that are innovative yet practical, forward-thinking yet reliable, and technically excellent yet human-centred. By balancing these elements, architects can design architectures that are not only robust and efficient today but also flexible, adaptable, and enduring for the future. This balanced approach ensures that organisations are well-equipped to meet their current needs and navigate the complexities of future challenges.

Architecture Standard Language

In Enterprise Architecture, clear and effective communication is paramount. The ability to convey complex architectural designs, principles, and strategies in a standardised, understandable format ensures that stakeholders across different functions—whether they are business leaders, developers, or project managers—are aligned and can make informed decisions. This chapter explores the importance of using standard languages to document and communicate architectural designs, the benefits of consistency in methods and deliverables, and discusses some of the most common architectural languages, such as Unified Modelling Language (UML) and ArchiMate. It also delves into their evolution and how they have shaped modern architectural practices.

Importance of Using Standard Language in Architecture

Foundational to architecture productivity is the need for a consistent set of **methods** and common **language** to close "The Great Divide" between Enterprise Architects and Solution Designers.

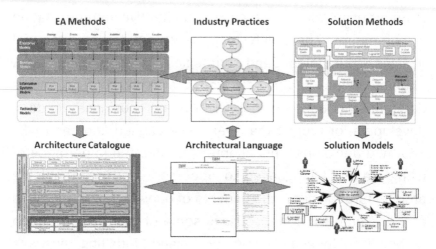

Figure 35: The bridge between EA and solution designs

The use of standardised languages in architecture is crucial for several reasons:

Clarity and Precision in Communication

Architectural designs often involve a complex web of interconnected components, systems, and processes that need to be clearly communicated to a diverse set of stakeholders. These stakeholders can range from highly technical experts, such as software developers and IT engineers, to non-technical business leaders who focus on strategic objectives and business value. Using a standardised language like Unified Modelling Language (UML) or ArchiMate allows architects to articulate intricate details with clarity and precision. For instance, when documenting a system's data flow or the structure of an application's components, employing a standard notation ensures a unified interpretation. Everyone, regardless of their technical background, understands the design in the same way, thereby reducing the chances of misinterpretation and misunderstandings. This common understanding is essential to ensure that all stakeholders, from project managers to developers, are on the same page regarding the project's goals and requirements.

Consistency in Methods and Deliverables

Standard languages play a crucial role in maintaining consistency across architectural practices within an organisation. They provide a uniform way to develop, document, and share architectural models, ensuring that all teams adhere to a coherent approach. This consistency is vital for several reasons. Firstly, it allows different parts of the architecture to be easily integrated, as the use of standardised symbols, terms, and diagrams ensures that all models are compatible. Secondly, it facilitates effective architecture reviews by providing a common basis for evaluation and feedback. Thirdly, it ensures compliance with established standards and best practices, reducing the risk of deviations that could compromise the architecture's integrity. Furthermore, consistent methods and deliverables simplify onboarding and training for new team members and stakeholders. When everyone is familiar with a single, standardised approach, there is less confusion, and the learning curve is significantly reduced, leading to more efficient project execution and collaboration.

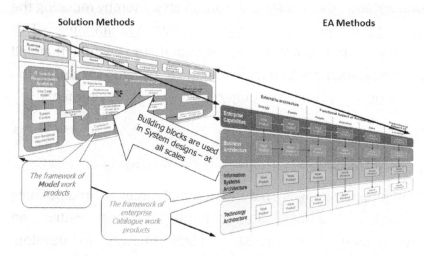

Figure 36: Consistency across views

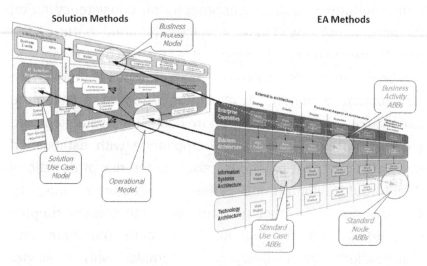

Figure 37: Consistency across models

Facilitates Collaboration and Reuse

Standard architectural languages act as a bridge between various stakeholders, such as architects, developers, business analysts, and project managers, enabling effective collaboration. When everyone involved in a project uses the same language and follows the same standards, it becomes easier to review work, identify potential issues, and provide constructive feedback. This common understanding fosters a collaborative environment where team members can easily share insights, suggestions, and improvements. Moreover, standardisation promotes the reuse of existing models, templates, and design patterns. Architects can leverage well-established models and frameworks rather than starting from scratch, saving significant time and effort. This reuse not only accelerates the development process but also ensures that proven best practices are consistently applied across different projects, leading to higher quality and more reliable outcomes.

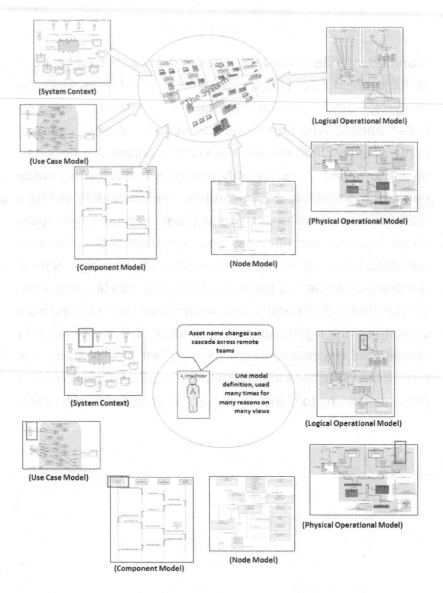

Figure 38: Consistency in object reference

Supports Governance and Compliance

Standardised languages are a fundamental component of governance and compliance in Enterprise Architecture. Governance ensures that architectural practices align with organisational goals and industry standards, and standardised languages play a critical role in achieving this alignment. By using recognised languages such as UML and ArchiMate, architects ensure that their designs conform to established standards and best practices, facilitating smoother architecture reviews and assessments. Standardisation makes it easier to audit architectural deliverables, as there is a clear and consistent basis for evaluating compliance with both internal policies and external regulations. This uniformity helps organisations avoid potential risks associated with non-compliance, such as financial penalties, security breaches, and operational inefficiencies. Additionally, it supports continuous improvement by providing a clear framework for identifying gaps, measuring performance, and implementing necessary changes.

Evolution of Architectural Language

The evolution of architectural languages in Enterprise Architecture has been driven by the need for more effective ways to design, document, and communicate complex systems in increasingly interconnected and digital environments. Initially developed to address software development challenges, these languages have expanded over time to encompass a broader range of concerns, from technical infrastructure to business processes and strategic goals. The journey from early modelling techniques to today's comprehensive frameworks like UML (Unified Modelling Language) and ArchiMate reflects the ongoing quest for precision, clarity, and adaptability in architecture.

Early Stages: From Flowcharts to Structured Design Methods

The earliest forms of architectural languages were simple **flowcharts and diagrams** used in the 1960s and 1970s to represent algorithms and basic program flows. These rudimentary tools were sufficient for small-scale software development projects but quickly became inadequate as systems grew more complex. The rise of structured programming in the 1970s led to the development of more sophisticated notations, such as **Data Flow Diagrams (DFDs)** and **Entity-Relationship Diagrams (ERDs)**, which provided a more robust way to model data relationships and system processes.

During this period, architectural languages were largely focused on representing technical aspects of software development. The primary goal was to create clear, unambiguous documentation that could be used by programmers and analysts to build reliable systems.

The Object-Oriented Revolution: Introduction of UML

The 1980s and 1990s marked a significant shift in architectural languages with the advent of **object-oriented programming (OOP)**. The need to model complex, object-oriented systems gave rise to a plethora of modelling techniques, each with its own notations and methodologies. This fragmentation created confusion and inconsistency within the industry. In response, three prominent figures—Grady Booch, Ivar Jacobson, and James Rumbaugh—known as the "Three Amigos," collaborated to develop a unified modelling approach. The result was the **Unified Modelling Language (UML)**, first standardised by the Object Management Group (OMG) in 1997.

UML represented a major leap forward, offering a comprehensive set of diagrams to model both the **structural and behavioural aspects** of systems. With its broad applicability, UML became the standard for modelling not only software systems but also business processes and other domains, bridging the gap between technical and business stakeholders. The language evolved through multiple versions, adding new types of diagrams, enhancing existing ones, and incorporating more sophisticated modelling concepts like **activity diagrams** and **sequence diagrams.**

Expanding the Scope: The Emergence of Enterprise Architecture Languages

As organisations began to recognise the importance of aligning IT with business strategy, there was a growing need for a language that could model not just software systems but entire enterprises. Enter **ArchiMate**, developed in the early 2000s by the **Open Group**. Unlike UML, which focuses heavily on software and systems, ArchiMate was designed specifically for **Enterprise Architecture**. It provided a structured language for describing the architecture of organisations across three main layers: **Business, Application, and Technology**.

ArchiMate's strength lies in its ability to provide a high-level view of an enterprise, illustrating how business processes, information systems, and technology infrastructure interact to achieve strategic objectives. Its layered approach made it particularly effective for enterprise architects who needed to communicate complex interdependencies and ensure alignment between IT and business strategies.

Modern Developments: Integration, Flexibility, and Digital Transformation

The digital transformation era has brought about new requirements and challenges for architectural languages.

Today's environments are characterised by rapid technological change, increased demand for agility, and the integration of disruptive technologies such as **cloud computing**, **microservices**, **artificial intelligence (AI)**, and the **Internet of Things (IoT)**. To adapt to these changes, both UML and ArchiMate have continued to evolve.

UML has incorporated extensions and profiles to model specialised domains, such as **real-time systems**, **cloud architectures**, and **IoT deployments**. It has also embraced integration with other frameworks and languages, providing more flexibility for architects to create holistic models that address both software and enterprise-level concerns.

ArchiMate has expanded its framework to include new elements that capture **strategy**, **motivation**, and **capability-based planning**, enabling architects to model not only the operational aspects of an enterprise but also its strategic direction and future capabilities. This evolution reflects a growing emphasis on **digital transformation** and **agile enterprise architecture**.

Future Directions: Towards Interoperability and Automation

The future of architectural languages is likely to be shaped by the need for greater **interoperability**, **automation**, and **collaborative capabilities**. As organisations increasingly adopt **DevOps**, **continuous integration/continuous deployment (CI/CD)** pipelines, and **AI-driven decision-making**, there is a push for architectural languages to integrate more seamlessly with development and operational tools.

Interoperability

Future architectural languages may focus on being interoperable with various development environments, modelling tools, and digital platforms. This would enable more seamless collaboration between different teams, tools, and methodologies.

Automation

There is a trend towards automating architectural analysis and governance, making it possible to enforce compliance and standards directly through tooling. For example, using model-driven development approaches, code generation, and automated impact analysis.

Collaboration

Modern architectural languages may incorporate more collaborative features, enabling real-time modelling, feedback, and updates. This aligns with the trend towards distributed teams and remote work environments.

Common Architectural Languages

Several standardised languages are commonly used in Enterprise Architecture for documenting and communicating architectural designs. Two of the most widely adopted languages are Unified Modelling Language (UML) and ArchiMate.

Unified Modelling Language (UML)

The **Unified Modelling Language (UML)** is one of the most widely used modelling languages in software engineering and system architecture. UML was developed in the mid-1990s by Grady Booch, Ivar Jacobson, and James Rumbaugh, who are known as the "Three Amigos." It was standardised by the Object Management Group (OMG) in 1997 and has since evolved into an internationally recognised standard for visualising, specifying, constructing, and documenting the artifacts of a system.

Key Features of UML

UML offers a set of graphical notations to create visual models of object-oriented software-intensive systems. It consists of various types of diagrams, including:

Structural Diagrams: Such as Class Diagrams, Object Diagrams, and Component Diagrams, which depict the static structure of the system.

Behavioural Diagrams: Such as Use Case Diagrams, Sequence Diagrams, and Activity Diagrams, which capture the dynamic aspects of the system.

Evolution of UML

Over the years, UML has evolved to support a wide range of applications beyond software engineering, including business process modelling, system engineering, and enterprise architecture. With its flexible and extensible nature, UML remains a preferred choice for modelling complex systems that require detailed documentation of both structure and behaviours.

ArchiMate

ArchiMate is a more recent modelling language that focuses specifically on Enterprise Architecture. Developed by the Open Group in the early 2000s, ArchiMate was designed to provide a clear and standardised framework for modelling enterprise architectures at various levels of abstraction. ArchiMate addresses some of the gaps that UML does not cover, particularly in the area of aligning IT with business processes and strategy.

Key Features of ArchiMate

ArchiMate offers a uniform representation for diagrams that describe enterprise architectures. It includes three core layers:

> **Business Layer**: Captures the business processes, roles, and functions within an organisation.
>
> **Application Layer**: Focuses on the application services and components that support business processes.
>
> **Technology Layer**: Details the infrastructure services, platforms, and networks that enable application services.

Evolution of ArchiMate

ArchiMate has undergone several iterations, with the most recent versions incorporating elements for modelling strategy, motivation, and physical implementation. It is now widely regarded as a comprehensive standard for enterprise architects who need to document the relationship between business processes and IT systems clearly.

Choosing the Right Language for Your Architecture

Selecting the right standard language for documenting and communicating architecture is a crucial decision that can significantly impact the effectiveness of your architecture practice. The choice of language depends on several factors, including the nature of the organisation, the complexity of the architecture, the specific use cases, and the stakeholders involved. The most common architectural languages, such as **Unified Modelling Language (UML)** and **ArchiMate**, each have their strengths and are suited for different scenarios. To make an informed choice, it's essential to understand the strengths and limitations of each language and how they align with the needs of your project and organisation.

Factors to Consider When Choosing an Architectural Language

Scope and Focus of the Architecture

The first consideration when choosing an architectural language is the scope and focus of the architecture you are developing. If your architecture is heavily focused on **software systems**, with a need for detailed modelling of software components, processes, and interactions, **UML** is a highly suitable choice. UML provides a rich set of diagram types to represent various aspects of software architecture, such as class diagrams for static structure, sequence diagrams for dynamic behaviours, and state diagrams for state transitions.

> **Example**: In a software development project where the primary goal is to design a microservices-based application, UML can be used to create **component diagrams** that show the structure of each microservice, **sequence diagrams** to depict the interactions between services, and **activity diagrams** to represent the workflows.

On the other hand, if the focus is on **Enterprise Architecture**, where the goal is to align IT with business strategy, **ArchiMate** is a more appropriate choice. ArchiMate provides a holistic view of the organisation, covering business processes, application services, and technical infrastructure, all within a single framework.

> **Example**: For a digital transformation initiative in a financial services company, ArchiMate can be used to model how new digital channels (like mobile banking apps) interact with existing back-office systems, ensuring alignment between new capabilities and core business processes.

Audience and Stakeholders

The choice of language also depends on the audience and stakeholders who will be using or reviewing the architectural models. UML, with its technical orientation, is well-suited for **development teams, software engineers, and technical architects** who need detailed views of the system's inner workings. It is especially useful in environments where technical rigor and precision are paramount.

In contrast, **ArchiMate** is designed to be more accessible to a broader audience, including **business stakeholders, enterprise architects, and decision-makers**. Its layered approach allows stakeholders to see high-level overviews and drill down into details as needed, making it ideal for **strategic planning** and **business-IT alignment** discussions.

> **Example:** In a meeting involving both technical teams and business leaders, ArchiMate can be used to present an overview of the organisation's capabilities, processes, and systems, allowing all participants to understand the architecture from their respective perspectives.

Complexity and Level of Detail

The complexity and level of detail required for the architectural documentation is another important factor. UML is highly detailed and suitable for representing **complex systems** where each component's behaviours, interaction, and data flow need to be meticulously documented. For projects that require a deep dive into technical aspects, such as the design of a high-frequency trading system or a real-time control system, UML's ability to capture **low-level details** is invaluable.

Conversely, ArchiMate provides a **higher-level view** and is better suited for projects where the goal is to understand the **interrelationships** between different architectural layers—business, application, and technology. ArchiMate can show how business processes are supported by applications and how those applications, in turn, rely on the underlying technology infrastructure.

Example: In an enterprise-wide cloud migration project, ArchiMate can be used to show how various business processes will be affected by the migration, how applications will interact with cloud services, and what changes will be needed in the technology infrastructure to support the migration.

Tooling and Integration with Existing Practices

The availability of tools and their integration with existing practices can also influence the choice of architectural language. UML is widely supported by various modelling tools, integrated development environments (IDEs), and **software development platforms**. It fits well into organisations that already use **model-driven development (MDD)** or **model-driven architecture (MDA)** approaches, where models are directly used to generate code.

> **Example**: An organisation using IBM Rational Rose or Visual Paradigm for UML modelling can seamlessly integrate these tools into their software development lifecycle, making UML a natural choice.

ArchiMate, meanwhile, is supported by several specialised EA tools like **Archi, Bizzdesign, Orbus Software, and Sparx Systems**, which provide robust features for modelling, analysis, and strategy development. These tools often come with built-in libraries for business processes, capabilities, and technology components, making it easier for architects to maintain **traceability** across different layers of the architecture.

> **Example**: An enterprise using the Bizzdesign tool can benefit from ArchiMate's integrated approach to modelling business, application, and technology layers, all while leveraging Bizzdesign's dashboarding and reporting capabilities for effective decision-making.

Need for Integration and Interoperability

If your architecture requires seamless **integration with existing systems** and adherence to specific **industry standards**, the choice of language becomes even more critical. UML, due to its maturity and widespread adoption, often integrates well with a variety of systems and processes. It is also highly customisable, which allows organisations to define profiles that cater to their unique requirements.

ArchiMate, with its focus on interoperability between business and IT, is ideal for organisations looking to implement **end-to-end enterprise architecture**. Its capability to model strategic motivations, business processes, applications, and technology layers in a single coherent framework facilitates alignment and interoperability.

Example: A government agency undergoing digital transformation may choose ArchiMate to ensure all aspects of their transformation—business processes, data management, applications, and infrastructure—are aligned and interoperable with other government systems and policies.

Combining UML and ArchiMate for Comprehensive Coverage

Many organisations find that using a combination of both UML and ArchiMate provides the best coverage for their needs. **ArchiMate** is used at the **strategic and operational levels** to ensure alignment between business and IT, while **UML** is used for **detailed technical modelling** at the software design and development stages. This hybrid approach allows organisations to benefit from both high-level overviews and detailed technical insights, creating a comprehensive, unified view of their architecture.

Example: In a large-scale ERP implementation, ArchiMate can be used to model the overall enterprise architecture, including business processes, application services, and technology infrastructure. UML can then be used to model the detailed design of specific modules, workflows, and data models within the ERP system, providing a full spectrum view from strategy to execution.

Choosing the right architectural language is not a one-size-fits-all decision. It requires a thorough understanding of the project's scope, the audience, the complexity of the systems being modelled, existing tools and practices, and the need for integration and interoperability. By carefully evaluating these factors and understanding the strengths of UML and ArchiMate, organisations can make informed decisions that enhance communication, consistency, collaboration, and governance across their architecture practices.

Architecture Building Blocks in Enterprise Architecture

Architecture that provide a modular, reusable approach to designing and implementing architecture solutions. They serve as the foundational elements that guide the development of complex systems by defining common functionalities, standards, and capabilities that are shared across various architectural layers. Architecture Building Blocks are critical to Enterprise Architecture because they provide a structured approach to ensure consistency, efficiency, and alignment with organisational goals and strategies.

This chapter explores the concept of Architecture Building Blocks, their significance in Enterprise Architecture, their role in fostering interoperability and scalability, and the benefits they bring to organisations aiming for efficient and sustainable IT and business solutions.

Understanding Architecture Building Blocks (ABBs)

Architecture Building Blocks (ABBs) are high-level, generic components of architecture that capture the fundamental business, information, application, and technology capabilities required to achieve business objectives. They serve as the building blocks for constructing **Solution Building Blocks (SBBs)**, which are specific implementations that fulfil the requirements defined by ABBs. ABBs can be conceptual, logical, or physical, depending on their level of abstraction and specificity. They are categorised into four primary domains:

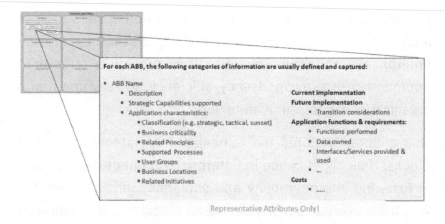

Figure 39: Architecture Building Blocks

Business Architecture Building Blocks (BABBs)

Represent the fundamental business capabilities, processes, and organisational structures that define how an organisation operates. Examples include customer relationship management (CRM), order processing, and supply chain management.

Information Architecture Building Blocks (IABBs)

Focus on data management and governance, data models, and the flow of information across systems and processes.

Examples include data repositories, data integration services, and metadata management frameworks.

Application Architecture Building Blocks (AABBs)

Define the software and application components required to support business processes and data management needs. Examples include enterprise resource planning (ERP) modules, content management systems (CMS), and API gateways.

Technology Architecture Building Blocks (TABBs)

Provide the technical infrastructure, platforms, and services needed to run applications and manage data. Examples include cloud platforms, network services, and cybersecurity frameworks.

Each ABB encapsulates a set of capabilities, standards, and guidelines that drive the design, implementation, and integration of specific architectural solutions. They provide a common vocabulary for architects, developers, and business stakeholders, enabling effective communication and collaboration across different teams.

Importance of Architecture Building Blocks in Enterprise Architecture

ABBs are vital to EA for several reasons:

Promote Reusability and Standardisation

One of the key advantages of ABBs is that they promote reusability and standardisation across the organisation. By defining reusable building blocks, organisations can avoid duplicating effort and ensure that solutions are built on a consistent foundation. For example, a data governance ABB can be reused across multiple projects to ensure data quality, consistency, and compliance. This reuse reduces development time, effort, and costs, leading to more efficient project delivery and maintenance.

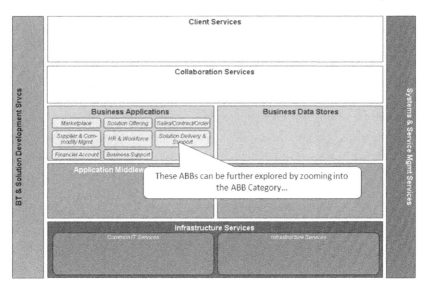

Figure 40: Standardised ABBs

Ensure Consistent Alignment with Strategic Goals

ABBs help ensure that architecture solutions are consistently aligned with the organisation's strategic goals and objectives. Since ABBs are defined at a high level and capture the core capabilities and standards required by the organisation, they provide a clear direction for designing solutions that align with business priorities. By leveraging ABBs, architects can create solutions that support key business drivers, such as enhancing customer experience, optimising operational efficiency, or driving innovation.

323

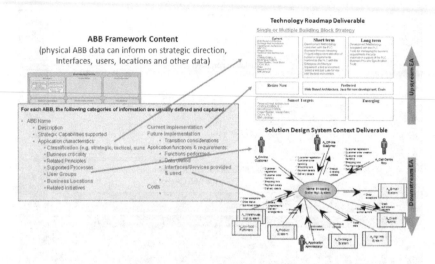

Figure 41: ABB aligned with Strategy

Facilitate Interoperability and Integration

In today's interconnected digital environment, the ability to integrate diverse systems and applications is crucial. ABBs define common standards and interfaces, ensuring that different solutions can work together seamlessly. For instance, an application integration ABB may define standard APIs, middleware, and messaging protocols, enabling disparate applications to communicate effectively. This interoperability reduces integration challenges, simplifies system landscapes, and enhances agility.

Support Scalability and Flexibility

ABBs are designed to be modular and flexible, allowing organisations to scale and adapt their architecture to changing business and technological needs. Because ABBs provide a well-defined structure, they make it easier to modify, extend, or replace components without disrupting the overall architecture. For example, a cloud platform ABB can be designed to support multiple cloud providers, allowing the organisation to scale its infrastructure as needed without vendor lock-in.

Improve Quality and Reduce Risks

ABBs incorporate best practices, standards, and compliance requirements, ensuring that architecture solutions are robust, secure, and compliant with regulatory guidelines. By using ABBs as the foundation for solution design, organisations can reduce the likelihood of errors, security vulnerabilities, and non-compliance risks. For example, a cybersecurity ABB may define the security controls and practices required for different types of data, helping to mitigate the risks associated with data breaches.

Enable Efficient Decision-Making and Governance

ABBs provide a structured approach to architecture development, making it easier for decision-makers to evaluate solutions, assess risks, and make informed decisions. Because ABBs are defined and governed centrally by the Architecture Office, they provide a single source of truth for standards, guidelines, and best practices. This central management enables effective governance, ensures that solutions are reviewed against established criteria, and facilitates compliance.

Accelerate Time-to-Market for Solutions

By leveraging predefined ABBs, organisations can accelerate the development and delivery of solutions. ABBs provide ready-to-use components and guidelines that simplify the design and implementation process. This accelerated time-to-market is particularly valuable in competitive environments where the ability to quickly deploy new capabilities can provide a significant advantage.

Implementing Architecture Building Blocks in Practice

Implementing ABBs effectively is essential to achieving a consistent, scalable, and interoperable architecture that aligns with organisational goals. This section explores the steps involved in implementing ABBs, the benefits they offer, and best practices to ensure successful deployment within an enterprise.

Steps to Implement ABBs in Enterprise Architecture

Implementing ABBs involves a systematic approach that ensures alignment with organisational goals and integrates well with the existing architectural framework. Below are the key steps involved:

Step 1: Define and Catalogue ABBs

The first step in implementing ABBs is to **define and catalogue** them clearly. This involves identifying the core capabilities, services, and components required across the different layers of architecture. The definitions should be comprehensive, capturing the essence of what each ABB represents, its purpose, and its interdependencies with other ABBs.

> **Example:** In a retail organisation, an ABB could be defined for a "Customer Relationship Management (CRM) Capability," detailing its functionalities (e.g., customer data management, interaction tracking, sales forecasting), its relation to other ABBs (e.g., integration with e-commerce platforms), and its underlying data requirements.

Once defined, ABBs should be catalogued in an **EA repository** or a centralised tool that allows easy access, searchability, and version control. This repository acts as the single source of truth for all ABBs within the organisation, ensuring consistency and reusability across different projects.

Step 2: Align ABBs with Business and IT Strategies

For ABBs to be effective, they must be aligned with both the business and IT strategies of the organisation. This requires collaboration between **enterprise architects**, **business stakeholders**, and **IT leaders** to ensure that the defined ABBs accurately reflect the strategic objectives and deliver tangible business value.

Example: In a financial services company, if the business strategy emphasises "customer-centricity" and "digital transformation," the ABBs should reflect capabilities like "Customer Data Integration" and "Omnichannel Digital Services," aligning IT services with customer experience goals.

During this phase, it is important to conduct **architecture reviews** to validate that the ABBs align with the organisation's reference models, architecture principles, and standards. Regular feedback loops with stakeholders help in refining and evolving ABBs to meet changing business needs.

Step 3: Develop Guidelines and Standards for ABB Usage

To ensure that ABBs are implemented consistently, organisations need to develop **guidelines and standards** for their usage. This includes defining the **naming conventions, documentation formats, and modelling notations** to be used for ABBs, as well as specifying the integration patterns, data standards, and security policies associated with each ABB.

Example: For an ABB representing "Data Analytics Capability," the guidelines could specify the use of ArchiMate for modelling, adherence to data privacy regulations like GDPR, and the use of specific data integration tools like Apache Kafka or Talend.

These guidelines help ensure that different teams across the organisation can implement ABBs in a way that is consistent, compatible, and compliant with organisational standards, thereby facilitating smooth integration and interoperability.

Step 4: Map ABBs to Solution Building Blocks (SBBs)

Once ABBs are defined and aligned with business strategy, the next step is to **map ABBs to Solution Building Blocks (SBBs)**. SBBs represent the concrete implementations of ABBs and specify the actual products, technologies, and processes used to realise the capabilities defined by the ABBs.

> **Example:** An ABB for "Customer Data Management" might map to an SBB that specifies the use of Salesforce CRM for customer data management, Apache Hadoop for big data processing, and REST APIs for data integration.

Mapping ABBs to SBBs provides a clear path from conceptual architecture to physical implementation, ensuring that all projects adhere to the strategic architecture blueprint while allowing flexibility in choosing specific solutions.

Step 5: Integrate ABBs into Solution Development and Delivery Processes

To make ABBs actionable, they need to be integrated into the **solution development and delivery processes**. This means embedding ABBs into the **architecture review processes, project initiation documents, and solution design templates**. Architects and project teams should refer to the ABBs repository when designing new solutions or making changes to existing ones.

> **Example:** During the development of a new e-commerce platform, the project team refers to the ABBs for "Payment Processing" and "Order Fulfilment" to ensure that the solution design aligns with enterprise-wide standards and best practices.

By integrating ABBs into the development lifecycle, organisations can ensure consistency in architecture, reduce redundancy, and facilitate faster decision-making by leveraging existing, well-defined building blocks.

Step 6: Monitor and Evolve ABBs Over Time

Finally, it is essential to **continuously monitor and evolve** ABBs to ensure they remain relevant and effective. This involves conducting regular reviews, assessing the usage and performance of ABBs in real projects, and gathering feedback from stakeholders to identify areas for improvement. As technology and business landscapes evolve, ABBs should be updated to reflect new requirements, emerging technologies, and changes in strategy.

> **Example:** If an ABB for "Mobile Application Development" initially focused on native development, it might evolve to include hybrid or progressive web app (PWA) development as these technologies become more prevalent.

Best Practices for Successful ABB Implementation

Implementing Architecture Building Blocks effectively requires a combination of strategic planning, stakeholder engagement, and continuous improvement to ensure alignment with organisational goals and the ever-evolving technological landscape. Following best practices can significantly enhance the success of ABB implementation, leading to a more robust, scalable, and cohesive enterprise architecture.

Ensure Stakeholder Engagement

One of the critical factors for successful ABB implementation is the active engagement of stakeholders from both **business and IT**. Engaging stakeholders throughout the ABB definition and implementation process ensures that the architectural building blocks align with strategic business goals and technological needs. This collaborative approach allows for better understanding and alignment between business objectives and IT capabilities, ensuring that ABBs provide tangible business value. Stakeholders should be involved in discussions and decision-making processes, including defining the scope of ABBs, prioritising capabilities, and validating alignment with business outcomes. Regular workshops, feedback sessions, and governance meetings can help maintain this engagement, fostering a culture of collaboration and shared ownership of the architecture.

Maintain a Centralised Repository

To ensure that ABBs are accessible and reusable across the organisation, it is essential to maintain a **centralised repository** or Enterprise Architecture tool that catalogues all defined ABBs. This repository should serve as the **single source of truth** for all architecture components, making it easy for different teams to search, access, and reference ABBs during solution design and development. A well-maintained repository promotes consistency and standardisation, reduces redundancy, and accelerates solution delivery by allowing architects and developers to leverage existing building blocks. Additionally, the repository should support version control, ensuring that the latest and most accurate versions of ABBs are always available. Automated workflows and notifications can also be integrated into the repository to keep teams informed of any updates or changes to the ABB library.

Integrate ABBs into EA Tooling

Ensure that ABBs are easily accessible to architects and developers, they should be integrated into EA tooling. This integration allows solution architects to reference ABBs directly from the tools they use, promoting adherence to standards and reducing the likelihood of errors.

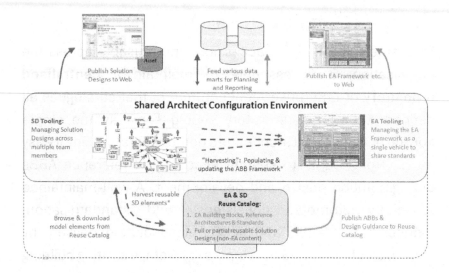

Figure 42: Integrate ABB into EA tools

Promote Training and Awareness

For ABBs to be effectively utilised in solution design and delivery, architects, developers, and project managers must be well-versed in how to use them. **Training programs** and **awareness campaigns** are crucial to ensure that all relevant stakeholders understand the purpose, benefits, and best practices associated with ABBs. Training should cover topics such as the principles of ABB design, the use of EA tools, and guidelines for integrating ABBs into solution architectures. Additionally, creating a **knowledge-sharing platform** or community of practice can help promote ongoing learning and the exchange of ideas and experiences among teams. By fostering a culture of continuous learning and improvement, organisations can enhance the effectiveness of their ABB implementations and drive better alignment with strategic objectives.

Regularly Review and Update ABBs

The business and technology landscapes are constantly evolving, and so too must the **ABBs** that form the foundation of an organisation's architecture. Establishing a **governance process** to review and update ABBs regularly is critical to ensure they remain relevant and aligned with current and future needs. This involves conducting periodic architecture reviews, assessing the effectiveness of existing ABBs, and making necessary adjustments based on feedback from stakeholders, changes in business strategy, or technological advancements. Regular updates help keep the ABB library fresh and relevant, preventing obsolescence and ensuring that ABBs continue to support the organisation's goals and objectives.

Measure and Monitor Usage

To continually improve the effectiveness of ABBs, it is essential to **measure and monitor** their usage in real projects. By tracking how frequently and effectively ABBs are used, organisations can gain valuable insights into their impact on solution design and delivery. Metrics such as reuse rates, project success rates, and compliance with architecture standards can help identify gaps, challenges, or opportunities for improvement. These insights should be used to refine and enhance the ABB library, ensuring it evolves in line with organisational needs and technological trends. Regular feedback loops and continuous monitoring also enable architects to identify best practices and share lessons learned across the organisation, further enhancing the value of ABBs.

Architecture Building Blocks (ABBs) are a critical element of effective Enterprise Architecture. They provide a modular, reusable approach to designing and implementing architecture solutions, ensuring alignment with strategic goals, promoting standardisation, enhancing interoperability, and reducing risks. By leveraging ABBs, organisations can build scalable, flexible, and high-quality architectures that support their business objectives and drive innovation. Effective implementation of ABBs involves defining clear standards, integrating them into EA tooling, communicating them to stakeholders, and continuously reviewing and updating them to meet evolving needs.

Architecture Documentation

This chapter aims to provide specific guidance on "how to develop and deliver architecture documentation throughout the project lifecycle". The target readership is:

- Project Solutions Architects;
- Project Managers and Project Teams;
- Program Managers.

As a generic term, the Solution Architect is responsible for architecture design and documentation in a project. This includes solution architecture, information architecture, and technical architecture.

In small-scale projects, a Solution Architect is responsible for all the requirements analysis and architecture in the project. For medium or large-scale projects, a number of Solution Architects may be involved, some responsible for working with the Business Analysts on business modelling and functional requirements analysis and documentation, others on data architecture, yet others responsible on application architecture, or technical architecture.

Other related people or teams who are relevant to this topic are: Project Business Architects or Business Analysts, Project Managers, and Design Leads.

The activities and templates used for architecture documentation are compliant with the Architecture Framework. They are also aligned with the Enterprise Architecture Metamodel.

Architecture modelling, documenting, and reporting activities should be carried out using the standard Enterprise Architecture toolsets.

Architecture Documentation: The Backbone of Successful Development Projects

A well-structured, clear, comprehensive, and accessible set of architecture documentation is essential for the success of application development projects. Architecture documents serve as a foundational tool that supports effective communication, validation, and management of system design throughout its lifecycle. They provide multiple stakeholders—ranging from project teams to service support personnel—with the necessary insights and guidelines needed to ensure a cohesive and well-aligned development process.

Key Roles of Architecture Documentation

Communication Across Stakeholders

Architecture documentation serves as a **critical communication vehicle** that conveys the system's design to various stakeholders at each stage of its evolution. These stakeholders include:

Project Teams

For developers and business analysts, architecture documentation provides a clear understanding of the business processes and requirements. It also shows how the application or system will meet these requirements. Furthermore, it provides the foundation for traceability throughout the project and the application/system lifecycle, ensuring alignment with the initial business goals.

Service/System or Application Designers and Implementers

The documentation establishes **inviolable constraints** (as well as **exploitable freedoms**) on the design and development activities. This ensures that the development aligns with the architectural vision and complies with the specified guidelines.

Testers and Integrators

For those responsible for quality assurance and system integration, the architecture dictates the expected black-box behaviours of individual components and how they fit together. This guidance is crucial for verifying system integrity and ensuring seamless integration.

Technical Managers

The architecture documentation helps technical managers form development teams that correspond to work assignments identified in the architecture. This alignment ensures that the right skills and resources are allocated to the right tasks, enhancing efficiency and productivity.

Project Managers

For project managers, architecture documentation is the basis for developing a **work breakdown structure (WBS)**, planning, allocating project resources, and tracking progress by the various teams. This provides a framework for managing project timelines and ensuring that all stakeholders are aligned.

Designers of Interoperable Systems

When designing systems that need to interoperate, the architecture defines the set of operations provided and required, along with the protocols for their operation. This clarity enables successful interoperation between different systems.

Validation and Refinement of Architectural Decisions

Architecture documentation serves as a **basis for up-front analysis**, helping validate architectural design decisions and identify any potential deficiencies early in the process. This proactive analysis allows for timely refinement or alteration of architectural decisions, reducing risks and improving the overall quality of the system.

Support for Service/Application Support Teams

For service and application support teams, architecture documentation provides a comprehensive overview of the system, including data flow, process flow, individual services or components, and their integration. This detailed insight is invaluable for efficient system analysis, troubleshooting, and diagnosis, enabling support teams to resolve issues more effectively.

Foundation for System Understanding and Reuse

Architecture documentation is often the **first artifact** consulted when trying to understand a system, even at detailed levels and service or component granularities. It serves as a crucial resource for:

Potential System Re-Engineering

Understanding the existing architecture is the first step in re-engineering a system. The documentation provides a clear view of the current state, enabling architects and engineers to plan improvements or redesigns effectively.

Asset and Service/Component Re-Use

Clear and detailed documentation of architecture allows for the identification of reusable assets, services, or components. This reuse can significantly reduce development time and costs while maintaining consistency across projects.

Architecture documentation is much more than a technical requirement; it is the backbone that supports all phases of a project, from conceptualisation to deployment and beyond. By providing a common language for all stakeholders, it ensures that everyone—from developers to project managers, to support teams—works cohesively towards a shared vision. Moreover, well-maintained documentation enables organisations to adapt, scale, and innovate more effectively by providing a solid foundation for future development, re-engineering, and optimisation.

What to Document

The architecture within an Enterprise Architecture Framework typically includes various interconnected domains. These domains cover different aspects of the organisation's systems and processes and provide a comprehensive view of how an organisation's IT architecture supports its business strategy and goals. The core components that should be documented in an enterprise architecture framework are:

- **Business Architecture**

- **Information Architecture**, which encompasses **Data Architecture** and **Application Architecture**

- **Technical Architecture**

Additionally, there is an overarching domain known as **Solution Architecture**, which integrates the business, information (data and application), and technical architectures to address specific business problems.

Business Architecture and Processes

Business Architecture lays the foundation for understanding and structuring business activities. It outlines accountability over these activities before diving into more detailed aspects such as processes, data, functions, organisation, systems, and applications. The Business Architecture documentation typically includes:

Layout of Business Domains

This involves mapping out business domains at various levels, detailing their assigned business processes, and highlighting the added value or "business case" for each domain.

Business Processes and Concepts

It includes descriptions of business processes and high-level data concepts that each business domain needs and is responsible for, enabling them to perform their activities effectively.

Interaction Among Processes and Activities

This section focuses on how different business processes and activities interact and work together to achieve organisational goals and strategies.

Key Elements of Business Architecture and Process Documentation

High-level Business Process Model

Outlines the hierarchical relationships between processes within the organisation.

As-Is Process Description

Documents the current state of processes.

Business Process Requirements

Details functional, informational, performance, constraints, and subjective requirements.

High-Level To-Be Process Design

Describes the future design of processes, building upon the As-Is state and aligning with business objectives.

Detailed To-Be Process Design

Provides a comprehensive, detailed design of the future state.

The business architecture deliverables serve as inputs for project requirement specifications, where both functional and non-functional requirements are analysed and documented.

Information Architecture: Data and Application Architecture

Information Architecture includes both **Data Architecture** and **Application Architecture**.

Data Architecture focuses on defining data and the requirements for managing data quality. It involves creating data models, exploring data solutions, and documenting data flows and interfaces. Key components of Data Architecture documentation include:

System Scope Overview: A concise overview of the system's scope regarding data and data management.

Business Data Glossary: Defines key data entities and ensures sufficient data design to support all processes.

CRUD Matrix: Maps business processes to data entities, showing Create, Read, Update, and Delete operations.

Logical Data Models: Application-specific models outlining data requirements, including security classifications, retention rules, and data quality standards.

CRUD Model: Defines how data can be manipulated in a database or system.

Data Flows and Interfaces: Outlines data flow requirements and designs for seamless integration.

Business Rules: Clearly states which rules are supported by data models, program/system code, or manual processes.

The goal of Data Architecture documentation is to promote data reusability across different processes within a project and across the organisation's systems and applications.

Application Architecture provides a structured overview of the system, describing the various integrated subsystems (application components), their associated data entities, and their relationships and interactions. This documentation includes:

Logical Overview of the System: A high-level view of the system or solution.

Application Services and Components: A list and detailed mapping of key application services and components to functional and business services.

Hierarchical View of Application Components: Breaks down components and shows dependencies among them.

Definition and Design of Each Component: Includes the component's functionality, internal and external properties, inputs and outputs, and interface specifications.

Data/Information Flow and Integration: Details the integration among these components, ensuring a seamless exchange of data.

Integration Architecture

Integration Architecture focuses on how different application components within a system interact and integrate with one another. Key aspects to document in Integration Architecture include:

Data/Information Flow: Describes how information flows among application components.

Interfaces and Interface Registry: Details the interfaces between components and maintains a registry of these interfaces.

Integration of Services and Components: Outlines the logical connections and integrations (e.g., ETL, EAI) among different services and components.

Technical Architecture

Technical Architecture addresses the technology required to support the application, including technical services, hardware, software, and infrastructure components (such as networks, communications, data storage, and security). Key components of Technical Architecture documentation are:

Logical Design of Technical Model Elements: Defines technical services and components in a logical view, without delving into physical design details.

Hardware and Software Specifications: Details the platforms, frameworks, and technical service building blocks.

Network and Infrastructure Overview: Describes network topology, geographical distribution, hosting environments, and other infrastructure-related details.

Non-Functional Requirements: Focuses on performance, resilience, storage, backup, availability, security (authentication, authorisation, auditing), and other non-functional aspects.

The emphasis for Technical Architecture is on conceptual and logical design, while the physical design and coding are typically left to project teams in the Design & Build stages.

Documenting architecture across these domains—Business, Information, Integration, and Technical—is essential for a comprehensive understanding of an organisation's systems and their alignment with business objectives. Each domain plays a critical role in ensuring that the architecture supports both current and future needs, fosters collaboration, and drives successful project outcomes. By maintaining detailed and structured documentation, organisations can achieve greater alignment, agility, and efficiency in their architectural endeavours.

Architecture Decision Document

An **Architecture Decision Document (ADD)** is a critical component in the practice of enterprise architecture. It captures the key architectural decisions made during a project, including the rationale behind each decision, the alternatives considered, and the implications of the chosen approach. ADDs provide a clear and structured way to document and communicate the decision-making process for the architecture team and other stakeholders. This ensures transparency, consistency, and accountability, which are essential for successful project execution and long-term architecture sustainability.

Importance of Architecture Decision Document

Provides Clear Justification for Decisions

ADDs provide a detailed rationale for each architectural decision, including the problem being addressed, the options considered, and the reasoning behind the chosen solution. This helps stakeholders understand why certain decisions were made, which is particularly important when decisions impact cost, timeline, or scope. By documenting the context and trade-offs, ADDs help prevent misunderstandings and miscommunications.

Enhances Transparency and Accountability

Having a documented record of architecture decisions makes the decision-making process transparent. This transparency fosters trust among stakeholders, including business leaders, IT teams, and external partners. It also establishes accountability by clearly identifying who was involved in making each decision and who is responsible for its outcomes.

Supports Knowledge Management and Continuity

ADDs act as a valuable knowledge base that can be referenced in the future. They help preserve the institutional memory of why certain architectural choices were made, which is crucial when team members change or when projects span long periods. ADDs ensure that new team members can quickly get up to speed on past decisions and maintain continuity in ongoing projects.

Facilitates Impact Analysis and Change Management

When changes are proposed in an architecture, ADDs provide a starting point for understanding the potential impact of those changes. By reviewing previous decisions, architects can assess how a proposed change might affect the architecture, identify dependencies, and make informed choices. This is particularly important in agile environments where changes are frequent, and quick decision-making is required.

Promotes Consistent Decision-Making

ADDs contribute to more consistent and standardised decision-making across projects. By capturing and sharing best practices and lessons learned, they help ensure that similar problems are addressed in similar ways across the organisation. This consistency reduces the likelihood of duplicated effort and prevents the team from repeating mistakes.

Examples of Architecture Decision Documents

Architecture Decision Documents can vary in format and content, but they generally include the following elements:

Decision Title	A concise, descriptive title for the decision.
Context	A brief explanation of the problem or situation that prompted the need for a decision. This section may include background information, business requirements, technical constraints, and any relevant dependencies.

Decision	A clear statement of the chosen option or solution. This section should summarise the decision in one or two sentences.
Rationale	A detailed explanation of why the decision was made. This section should cover the criteria used for evaluation, the alternatives considered, and the pros and cons of each option.
Implications	An analysis of the impact of the decision, including technical, business, operational, and financial aspects. This section should also address potential risks and how they will be mitigated.
Assumptions	Any assumptions made during the decision-making process that may influence the outcome.
Status	The current status of the decision (e.g., proposed, approved, implemented).
Reviewers and Approvers	A list of stakeholders who reviewed and approved the decision, along with the dates of approval.

Example 1: Choosing a Cloud Provider

Decision Title	Selection of Cloud Provider for the New E-Commerce Platform
Context	The organisation is migrating its e-commerce platform to the cloud to improve scalability, reduce operational costs, and enhance customer experience. Several cloud providers are available, each with different offerings, pricing models, and support options.
Decision	The organisation will use AWS as the cloud provider for the new e-commerce platform.
Rationale	AWS was chosen due to its comprehensive service offerings, global availability, competitive pricing, and robust security and compliance capabilities. Alternatives such as Microsoft Azure and Google Cloud were considered, but they did not provide the same level of flexibility and support for the specific needs of our e-commerce platform.
Implications	This decision will require team members to be trained on AWS services and tools. Additionally, there will be a need to refactor some existing applications to ensure compatibility with AWS services. The estimated cost savings over five years are projected to be 25% compared to the current on-premises solution.

Assumptions	The assumption is that AWS will continue to provide competitive pricing and high service availability.
Status	Approved
Reviewers and Approvers	Ian Loe (CIO), , Approved on March 15, 2024.

Example 2: Selecting a Microservices Architecture Pattern

Decision Title	Adoption of Microservices Architecture for Customer Data Management.
Context	The customer data management system needs to be modernised to support real-time data processing, scalability, and easier integration with third-party services. The current monolithic architecture presents challenges in terms of scalability and maintainability.
Decision	The system will be re-architected using a microservices architecture pattern.
Rationale	The microservices architecture was chosen because it offers better modularity, flexibility, and scalability. It allows for independent development and deployment of services, which aligns with the organisation's DevOps and CI/CD practices. Alternative options, such as refactoring the monolith or adopting a modular monolith approach, were considered but did not provide the same level of scalability and agility.

Implications	This decision will involve additional complexity in terms of service orchestration, inter-service communication, and data consistency. A containerisation platform (e.g., Kubernetes) will be used to manage microservices deployment, and team members will require training on containerisation and microservices design principles.
Assumptions	It is assumed that the team will have the necessary skills and resources to implement and manage a microservices architecture.
Status	Proposed
Reviewers and Approvers	John Smith (Lead Architect), Jane Doe (Project Manager), Under Review.

An Architecture Decision Document (ADD) is a powerful tool for ensuring that architecture decisions are made transparently, consistently, and with a full understanding of their implications. By providing a structured way to capture the context, rationale, and impact of each decision, ADDs help organisations manage complexity, ensure alignment with business goals, and foster collaboration among stakeholders. Properly maintained and utilised, ADDs become a critical asset for effective architecture governance and knowledge management.

Architecture Compliance Checklist

An **Architecture Compliance Checklist** is an essential tool for ensuring that architectural designs, implementations, and processes adhere to the organisation's established standards, principles, and policies. This checklist acts as a structured guide for architects, project managers, and stakeholders to evaluate whether a proposed architecture aligns with the Enterprise Architecture framework, meets regulatory and industry requirements, and supports the organisation's strategic goals. A well-defined architecture compliance checklist helps maintain consistency, reduce risks, and ensure quality across the architecture lifecycle.

Key Components of an Architecture Compliance Checklist

Below are some of the key components of the Architecture Compliance Checklist that you should develop for your organisation as part of any project architecture documentation.

Alignment with Enterprise Architecture Principles and Standards

Ensuring alignment with the organisation's established Enterprise Architecture principles is fundamental to maintaining a cohesive and effective architecture. This involves verifying that the architecture complies with principles such as modularity, interoperability, scalability, and security.

Modularity ensures that components are designed to be independent and interchangeable, enhancing flexibility and maintainability. Interoperability focuses on the seamless exchange of information between systems, which is crucial for operational efficiency. Scalability and security ensure that the architecture can handle growth and is protected against threats. Furthermore, the architecture must adhere to relevant standards, including naming conventions, documentation formats, and approved technology stacks. These standards create a uniform approach, reducing complexity and facilitating collaboration across teams.

Integration with Existing Systems and Services

Successful integration with existing systems and services is critical for maintaining a coherent IT ecosystem. The proposed architecture must seamlessly integrate with current systems, services, and data repositories to avoid silos and ensure smooth operations. Compatibility with the current IT landscape—including APIs, data formats, middleware, and integration platforms—must be confirmed. This involves checking that data formats are consistent, middleware is compatible, and integration platforms support the desired communication. Adherence to established integration patterns, such as Service-Oriented Architecture (SOA) or microservices, ensures that new components fit well within the existing environment. These patterns provide guidelines for how different systems should interact, helping to maintain consistency and reduce integration complexity.

357

Consistency Across Architectural Domains

Consistency across different architectural domains—Business Architecture, Information Architecture (including Data and Application Architectures), and Technical Architecture—is essential for a unified architecture. This involves validating that each domain aligns with the overall architecture strategy and supports the organisation's objectives. Dependencies and interactions among these domains must be well-documented to provide a clear understanding of how changes in one domain may impact others. For instance, a change in the business process may require adjustments in the data architecture. Ensuring consistency across these domains helps prevent conflicts and redundancies, facilitating smoother implementation and maintenance.

Compliance with Regulatory and Security Requirements

Compliance with regulatory and security requirements is a non-negotiable aspect of any architecture. The architecture must meet relevant regulatory requirements such as GDPR, PDPA, PDPO, HIPAA, or PCI-DSS, along with any industry-specific standards. This ensures that the organisation avoids legal penalties and maintains its reputation. Additionally, robust security controls must be in place, including data encryption, identity and access management (IAM), and incident response plans. These controls protect against data breaches and other security threats. Adherence to the organisation's security policies, such as data privacy, retention, and classification rules, is also essential. This includes ensuring that data is stored securely, accessed only by authorised personnel, and retained for appropriate periods.

Use of Approved Technology and Tools

The architecture should utilise only the technologies, frameworks, and tools that have been approved by the organisation's technology roadmap and standards. This helps maintain a standardised environment, making it easier to manage and support. Any deviations or exceptions from the approved technology list must be well-documented, justified, and approved by the relevant governance body. This process ensures that exceptions are carefully considered and do not introduce unnecessary risk or complexity.

Performance, Scalability, and Resilience Requirements

Evaluating whether the architecture meets the organisation's non-functional requirements (NFRs) related to performance, scalability, availability, and resilience is crucial. The design must include measures to handle load balancing, fault tolerance, disaster recovery, and capacity planning. These considerations ensure that the architecture can perform well under varying loads, recover quickly from failures, and scale to meet future demands. Meeting these requirements helps maintain system reliability and user satisfaction.

Documentation and Artifact Completeness

Comprehensive and up-to-date documentation is vital for understanding, maintaining, and evolving the architecture. All necessary architectural documentation and artifacts must be complete and stored in the designated architecture repository or tool. This includes business processes, data models, and technical components. Clear linkages and references among these artifacts help stakeholders understand the interdependencies and relationships within the architecture. Proper documentation facilitates effective communication and decision-making throughout the project lifecycle.

Risk Management and Mitigation

Identifying potential risks associated with the proposed architecture, such as technological obsolescence, integration challenges, or security vulnerabilities, is a key component of risk management. Once identified, risk mitigation strategies must be in place and documented to ensure that risks are managed proactively. There should also be plans for regular risk assessments throughout the project lifecycle. This ongoing evaluation helps identify new risks and adjust mitigation strategies as needed.

Review and Approval Processes

The architecture must undergo all required reviews, including peer reviews, domain reviews, and governance board approvals. This thorough review process ensures that the architecture is robust, compliant, and aligned with organisational goals. Any feedback or concerns raised during the review process must be addressed and documented to demonstrate due diligence and continuous improvement.

Monitoring and Feedback Mechanisms

Mechanisms for continuous monitoring of the architecture's performance, compliance, and alignment with strategic objectives are essential for ongoing success. This includes monitoring tools and processes that provide real-time insights into how the architecture is functioning. Additionally, there must be a feedback loop to capture lessons learned and continuously improve the architecture and compliance processes. This iterative approach helps adapt the architecture to evolving needs and ensures it remains effective and relevant.

Below is an example of an Architecture Compliance Checklist that can be used in a project:

Architecture Compliance Checklist

Project Name: [Enter Project Name]

Architect: [Enter Architect Name]

Date: [Enter Date]

Reviewer: [Enter Reviewer Name]

1. Alignment with Enterprise Architecture Principles and Standards

Criteria	Compliant (Yes/No)	Comments /Notes
Does the architecture align with the EA principles (e.g., modularity, scalability, interoperability)?	[ ] Yes [ ] No	
Are all naming conventions and documentation standards followed?	[ ] Yes [ ] No	
Does the architecture align with the approved technology stack and roadmap?	[ ] Yes [ ] No	

2. Integration with Existing Systems and Services

Criteria	Compliant (Yes/No)	Comments /Notes
Is there seamless integration with existing systems, services, and data repositories?	[ ] Yes [ ] No	
Are integration patterns (e.g., SOA, microservices) consistent with EA guidelines?	[ ] Yes [ ] No	
Are APIs, data formats, and middleware properly defined and documented?	[ ] Yes [ ] No	

3. Consistency Across Architectural Domains

Criteria	Compliant (Yes/No)	Comments/Notes
Is there consistency between Business, Information (Data and Application), and Technical Architectures?	[ ] Yes [ ] No	
Are the dependencies and interactions among these domains clearly defined and documented?	[ ] Yes [ ] No	

4. Compliance with Regulatory and Security Requirements

Criteria	Compliant (Yes/No)	Comments/Notes
Does the architecture comply with regulatory requirements (e.g., GDPR, PDPA, HIPAA, PCI-DSS)?	[ ] Yes [ ] No	
Are data encryption, IAM, and security controls in place?	[ ] Yes [ ] No	
Are security policies (data privacy, retention, classification) adhered to?	[ ] Yes [ ] No	

5. Use of Approved Technology and Tools

Criteria	Compliant (Yes/No)	Comments/Notes
Are the technologies, frameworks, and tools on the approved list?	[ ] Yes [ ] No	
Are any deviations or exceptions documented and approved?	[ ] Yes [ ] No	

6. Performance, Scalability, and Resilience Requirements

Criteria	Compliant (Yes/No)	Comments/Notes
Does the architecture meet performance and scalability requirements?	[ ] Yes [ ] No	
Are measures for load balancing, fault tolerance, and disaster recovery defined?	[ ] Yes [ ] No	

7. Documentation and Artifact Completeness

Criteria	Compliant (Yes/No)	Comments/Notes
Is all necessary architecture documentation complete and up-to-date?	[ ] Yes [ ] No	
Are cross-references between different artifacts provided?	[ ] Yes [ ] No	

8. Risk Management and Mitigation

Criteria	Compliant (Yes/No)	Comments/Not es
Are potential risks identified, and mitigation strategies documented?	[ ] Yes [ ] No	
Is there a plan for regular risk assessment throughout the project lifecycle?	[ ] Yes [ ] No	

9. Review and Approval Processes

Criteria	Compliant (Yes/No)	Comments/Not es
Has the architecture undergone all required peer reviews and governance board approvals?	[ ] Yes [ ] No	
Are feedback and concerns from the review process documented and addressed?	[ ] Yes [ ] No	

10. Monitoring and Feedback Mechanisms

Criteria	Compliant (Yes/No)	Comments/Not es
Are mechanisms in place for continuous monitoring of architecture performance and compliance?	[ ] Yes [ ] No	
Is there a feedback loop for capturing lessons learned and improving processes?	[ ] Yes [ ] No	

Sign-Off and Approval

Reviewer	Date	Approval Status
[Enter Reviewer Name]	[Enter Date]	[ ] Approved [ ] Rejected
Comments		

Benefits of Using an Architecture Compliance Checklist

Using an **Architecture Compliance Checklist** offers several significant benefits that enhance the overall effectiveness of enterprise architecture within an organisation. Firstly, it promotes **standardisation** by ensuring consistent architectural practices across different projects and teams. This uniformity helps in maintaining alignment with the organisation's strategic goals and reduces the complexity associated with managing diverse architectural approaches.

Secondly, the checklist aids in **risk mitigation** by helping to identify potential risks early in the design process and establishing the necessary controls to mitigate them. This proactive approach to risk management ensures that issues are addressed before they escalate into more significant problems.

Another critical benefit is **quality assurance**. By following a structured checklist, architects can ensure that their designs are robust, secure, and aligned with the organisation's business objectives. The checklist serves as a quality control mechanism, helping to validate that all essential criteria are met before implementation.

Moreover, the checklist enhances **efficiency** by streamlining the review process. It provides a clear and concise framework for assessing compliance, reducing the time and effort required for reviews and approvals.

Finally, the checklist fosters **accountability** by documenting the compliance status and decisions made throughout the architectural process. This documentation provides a transparent trail for governance and auditing purposes, ensuring that all architectural activities are traceable and justifiable. Together, these benefits make the Architecture Compliance Checklist an indispensable tool for effective enterprise architecture management.

Architecture Management and Ensuring Alignment

The role of a Solution Architect involves not only designing solutions but also ensuring that these solutions are aligned and integrated with the broader enterprise architecture. This requires a meticulous approach to managing architecture documentation and ensuring compliance with established standards. The Solution Architect must oversee several key tasks to maintain consistency and quality across the architecture landscape

Ensure Comprehensive Coverage and Consistency Across Architectures

The Solution Architect must ensure that there is comprehensive coverage and consistency among the different layers of architecture—**Business Architecture (BA), Information Architecture (IA), and Technical Architecture (TA)**. Each of these layers should align and work cohesively to support the overall business strategy. This involves coordinating with various stakeholders and ensuring that each layer is developed in harmony with the others, avoiding any gaps or overlaps.

Establish Links and References Among Architecture Artifacts

It is crucial to create clear links and references between different architectural artifacts, including those within the **Business, Information, and Technical Architectures**. These interconnections help provide a holistic view of the architecture, showing how each part relates to and impacts the others. Proper linking ensures that changes in one area are understood in the context of the entire architecture, facilitating better decision-making and impact analysis.

Maintain Documented Artefacts with Cross-References

All architecture documentation and artifacts must be well-documented, with comprehensive cross-references provided among them. This ensures that each architectural element can be easily navigated and understood within the broader context. For example, a business process in the BA should reference the data models in the IA that it relies on, and the supporting infrastructure in the TA. This interconnected documentation aids in understanding dependencies and relationships within the architecture.

Load Artefacts into Standard Tools and Repositories

To maintain consistency and accessibility, all architecture documentation and artifacts should be uploaded to the organisation's standard architecture tools and repositories. This centralised storage ensures that all stakeholders have access to the most up-to-date and accurate architectural information. It also supports version control, audit trails, and collaborative review processes.

Ensure Compliance with Reference Models, Metamodels, and Standards

 Solution Architects must ensure that their work complies with the enterprise's **EA reference models, EA metamodels, architecture standards, principles, and policies**. These frameworks provide the foundational guidelines that ensure architectural consistency, quality, and alignment with the organisation's strategic goals. Regular checks for compliance help to maintain architectural integrity and avoid deviations that could lead to misalignment or inefficiencies.

Document Any Deviations or Step-Outs from Standards

When a deviation from the established standards or principles is necessary, it must be carefully noted and documented. This "step-out" process involves providing a clear rationale for why a deviation is required, along with an assessment of its potential impact. Documenting these step-outs ensures transparency and enables stakeholders to make informed decisions about accepting or mitigating deviations.

Prepare for Architecture Review in Collaboration with the Project Manager

Finally, the Solution Architect must collaborate closely with the Project Manager to prepare for the **Architecture Review**. This review is a critical checkpoint where the proposed architecture is evaluated for its compliance, alignment, and overall feasibility. By working together, the Solution Architect and Project Manager can ensure that all necessary documentation, justifications, and plans are ready for scrutiny, enhancing the likelihood of a successful review.

Effective architecture management requires a systematic approach to documenting, linking, and maintaining architectural artifacts across all domains—Business, Information, and Technical. By ensuring compliance with enterprise standards, documenting deviations, and preparing thoroughly for architecture reviews, Solution Architects play a vital role in aligning solutions with organisational goals and maintaining the integrity of the overall enterprise architecture.

Governance in Enterprise Architecture

Effective governance is a cornerstone of any successful Enterprise Architecture management. It provides a structured approach to decision-making, ensures alignment with strategic goals, and enforces compliance with established standards and principles. Governance in Enterprise Architecture is not a one-time activity but an ongoing process that involves multiple stakeholders, from executive leadership to project teams, working together to deliver value to the organisation. This chapter explores the proposed governance structure, focusing on the relationships between the Executive Steering Group, the Architecture Office, the Project Teams, and the Technical Review Board. It also delves into the roles, responsibilities, and deliverables of each component within the governance framework, ensuring a cohesive and efficient architecture process.

Governance Structure in Enterprise Architecture

The governance structure in Enterprise Architecture is designed to provide oversight, ensure alignment with organisational objectives, and manage the lifecycle of architectural solutions. The key components of this governance structure include:

1. **Executive Steering Group**

2. **Architecture Office**

3. **Project Teams**

4. **Technical Review Board**

Each of these entities plays a distinct role in the governance process, contributing to a robust and well-managed architecture.

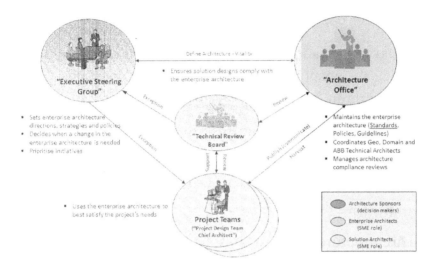

Figure 43: Relationship between groups in EA governance

Executive Steering Group (ESG)

The **Executive Steering Group** is at the top of the Enterprise Architecture governance structure and provides strategic oversight and decision-making authority. Comprised of senior executives from various business units and IT leaders, the ESG is responsible for:

- **Setting Strategic Direction**: The ESG aligns the Enterprise Architecture with the organisation's overall business strategy, ensuring that architecture initiatives support long-term goals.

- **Prioritisation and Funding**: The committee decides which architectural projects and initiatives receive funding and resources based on strategic priorities and business impact.

- **Governance and Compliance**: It oversees governance policies, ensuring that architecture principles and standards are enforced across the organisation.

Deliverables: The ESG produces strategic directives, funding approvals, prioritisation guidelines, and high-level governance policies.

Architecture Office

The **Architecture Office** acts as the central hub for Enterprise Architecture governance, responsible for developing, maintaining, and enforcing architecture standards and guidelines. It comprises enterprise architects and subject matter experts who focus on Architecture and Technology standards. The Architecture Office is tasked with:

- **Optimising the Architecture Review Process**: The Architecture Office ensures that the architecture review process is efficient and integrated into the end-to-end solution lifecycle. This includes developing checklists that clarify where standards should be reviewed for relevance at each stage of the solution lifecycle.

- **Central Management of Standards**: The Architecture Office centrally manages enterprise-wide standards, providing a single source for definitions and communication. This centralisation makes it easier for stakeholders to find, read, and comply with standards.

- **Method Adoption**: The Architecture Office is responsible for promoting method adoption where relevant architecture principles are referenced, and standards are identified. This ensures that solutions are aligned with the organisation's strategic goals.

Deliverables: The Architecture Office delivers architecture standards, review checklists, compliance reports, and recommendations for updating or retiring principles and standards.

Project Teams

Project Teams are responsible for the implementation of solutions that adhere to the architecture standards and principles defined by the Architecture Office. These teams include solution architects, developers, business analysts, and other stakeholders involved in delivering IT projects. Their roles and responsibilities include:

- **Adhering to Standards**: Project Teams are required to align their solutions with the established Architecture & Technology standards and ensure compliance throughout the development lifecycle.

- **Collaboration with the Architecture Office**: Project Teams collaborate closely with the Architecture Office to ensure that their projects align with EA standards and principles. This collaboration often involves regular check-ins and reviews.

- **Feedback and Improvement**: They provide feedback to the Architecture Office regarding the relevance and practicality of the standards, suggesting improvements where necessary.

Deliverables: Project Teams deliver compliant solutions, project documentation, and feedback on standards and processes.

Technical Review Board (TRB)

The **Technical Review Board** is a cross-functional body consisting of senior architects and technical experts. It serves as a checkpoint for evaluating architectural solutions to ensure compliance with standards, principles, and policies. The TRB is responsible for:

- **Conducting Architecture Reviews**: The TRB conducts regular architecture reviews at various stages of the project lifecycle to ensure that the solutions meet the established A&T standards.

- **Assessing Compliance and Risks**: The TRB evaluates the level of compliance with architecture standards and identifies any potential risks or deviations that need to be addressed.

- **Providing Guidance and Approvals**: The TRB provides guidance to Project Teams and the AO, offering recommendations for improvements and approving solutions that meet compliance requirements.

Deliverables: The TRB provides review findings, compliance assessments, risk reports, and approval decisions.

End-to-End Architecture Governance Process

An effective Enterprise Architecture governance process is focused on optimising architecture reviews and the solution lifecycle into an integrated, end-to-end process. Key elements of this process include:

Method Adoption and Standards Compliance

The governance process ensures that relevant architecture principles are referenced, and standards are identified early in the solution lifecycle. This approach helps in maintaining consistency and compliance.

Checklists for Lifecycle Reviews

The process includes checklists that clarify where in the solution lifecycle standards should be reviewed for relevance to a project. This ensures that standards are applied appropriately and consistently.

Centralised Communication of Standards

The governance framework mandates that all standards are centrally managed and communicated via a single source, such as a dedicated website. This centralisation simplifies access and ensures that stakeholders are aware of the standards they need to follow.

Architecture & Technology Standards in EA Tooling

To support Solution Architects, Architecture & Technology standards should be accessible directly from Enterprise Architecture tooling. This proximity to where the architects work ensures that standards are readily available and applied correctly.

Regular Refresh and Retirement of Principles

Governance involves regularly refreshing and retiring principles that are no longer relevant to the business and IT strategy. This ensures that the EA remains aligned with evolving organisational goals.

Measuring Compliance and Progress

To ensure that the governance framework is effective, it is essential to measure progress towards realising architecture principles, compliance with standards, and the realisation of Architecture Building Blocks (ABBs). This measurement involves:

- **Tracking Compliance Levels**: Regular audits and reviews are conducted to assess the degree of compliance with established standards.

- **Assessing Impact on Strategic Goals**: The effectiveness of the architecture in contributing to strategic goals is evaluated.

- **Continuous Improvement**: The governance framework is continuously refined based on feedback from Project Teams, TRB reviews, and ESC directives.

Governance in Enterprise Architecture is a multi-layered process involving various roles and responsibilities, from strategic oversight by the Executive Steering Committee to detailed compliance checks by the Technical Review Board. A well-structured governance framework ensures that architecture initiatives are aligned with organisational goals, standards are consistently applied, and risks are effectively managed. By focusing on optimising processes, ensuring clarity in standard application, and providing centralised communication, Enterprise Architecture governance creates a strong foundation for delivering value through architecture.

The Future of Enterprise Architecture

The future of Enterprise Architecture will be shaped by several emerging trends, each driven by the evolving needs of businesses and technological advancements. As organisations strive to remain competitive, efficient, and compliant in an ever-changing landscape, Enterprise Architecture will need to adapt to these new paradigms. Let's expand on each of these key areas that will define the future of Enterprise Architecture.

Agility and Flexibility

In a rapidly changing business environment, **agility and flexibility** will be paramount for Enterprise Architecture. This trend reflects the growing need for organisations to respond swiftly to market changes, customer demands, and technological advancements. Traditional rigid architectures will no longer suffice; instead, architects will need to design modular, scalable, and adaptable architectures that can evolve as business needs change.

Embracing Agile Methodologies

Enterprise Architecture will increasingly align with agile development methodologies, promoting iterative design, continuous integration, and rapid deployment. This shift enables organisations to test and implement changes quickly, fostering innovation and reducing time-to-market.

Microservices and API-First Approaches

Adopting microservices architecture and API-first design principles will be essential. These approaches allow for greater flexibility in how systems are built and maintained, enabling organisations to replace, upgrade, or integrate new components without disrupting the entire architecture.

Cloud-Native and Hybrid Architectures

Leveraging cloud-native and hybrid cloud architectures will be a common strategy to enhance flexibility. These architectures allow businesses to scale resources up or down as needed and deploy applications across various environments seamlessly.

Digital Transformation

Digital transformation is an ongoing journey for many organisations, and Enterprise Architecture will be at the forefront of guiding and managing this process. Enterprise Architecture will act as a strategic enabler, ensuring that digital initiatives are aligned with business objectives and integrated into the existing architectural landscape.

Integration of Emerging Technologies

Architects will need to incorporate a range of new technologies—such as cloud computing, artificial intelligence (AI), machine learning (ML), and the Internet of Things (IoT)—into their architectural designs. This involves understanding how these technologies can enhance business capabilities and designing architectures that support their integration.

Customer-Centric Design

Digital transformation is often driven by the need to enhance customer experience. Enterprise Architecture will focus on designing architectures that enable seamless customer interactions, personalisation, and real-time engagement through digital channels.

Automation and Intelligent Systems

The rise of AI and ML will lead to more automated and intelligent systems within the architecture. This includes leveraging AI for predictive analytics, decision-making, and process automation to drive efficiency and innovation.

Data-Centric Architecture

In the digital age, **data has become a strategic asset** for organisations, driving decision-making, innovation, and competitive advantage. As a result, Enterprise Architecture will increasingly adopt a data-centric approach to maximise the value of data.

Data Governance and Management

Ensuring data quality, consistency, and security will be central to Enterprise Architecture. This involves implementing robust data governance frameworks, data catalogues, and master data management (MDM) systems that standardise and govern data across the organisation.

Scalable Data Architectures

With the exponential growth of data, Enterprise Architecture will need to design scalable data architectures capable of handling large volumes of structured and unstructured data. This includes leveraging big data technologies, cloud-based data lakes, and real-time data processing frameworks like Apache Kafka and Apache Flink.

Advanced Analytics and AI Integration

To support advanced analytics and AI capabilities, EA will focus on designing architectures that enable seamless data integration and accessibility. This includes ensuring data availability across different platforms and optimising data pipelines for analytics workloads.

Security and Compliance

As cyber threats become more sophisticated and regulations more stringent, **security and compliance** will play a more critical role in Enterprise Architecture. EA will need to embed security principles into every layer of the architecture, ensuring robust protection against evolving threats and compliance with regulatory standards.

Zero Trust Architecture

The adoption of a Zero Trust approach—where every access request is verified, regardless of its origin—will become a cornerstone of secure architecture. This involves implementing strong identity and access management (IAM), encryption, and continuous monitoring to safeguard critical assets.

Proactive Threat Detection and Response

Enterprise Architecture will integrate advanced security solutions such as AI-driven threat detection, Security Information and Event Management (SIEM) systems, and automated incident response to proactively address potential security breaches.

Compliance-Driven Architecture

Ensuring compliance with regulations like GDPR, PDPA, PDPO, HIPAA, and CCPA will require architectures that can enforce data privacy, enable audit trails, and provide robust data protection measures. Compliance as code would be an integral part of any design.

Sustainability and Green IT

As organisations become more aware of their **environmental impact**, there is a growing emphasis on designing sustainable and energy-efficient architectures. **Green IT** practices will become integral to Enterprise Architecture, reflecting a commitment to sustainability and corporate social responsibility.

Energy-Efficient Data Centres

Enterprise Architecture will need to consider energy consumption and efficiency when designing data centres and IT infrastructure. This involves optimising server utilisation, leveraging virtualisation, and using energy-efficient cooling and power systems to reduce carbon footprints.

Cloud Optimisation and Green Computing

By optimising cloud usage and leveraging serverless computing models, organisations can reduce waste and improve efficiency. Enterprise Architecture will focus on cloud cost management and resource optimisation to ensure sustainable cloud operations.

Sustainable Software Development

Beyond infrastructure, Enterprise Architecture will also promote sustainable software development practices, such as writing efficient code, reducing technical debt, and adopting practices like Continuous Integration/Continuous Deployment (CI/CD) that minimise waste.

The future of Enterprise Architecture is dynamic and multifaceted, driven by the need for agility, digital transformation, data-centricity, security, and sustainability. As these trends continue to evolve, architects must adapt by embracing new technologies, frameworks, and practices that enable organisations to thrive in a rapidly changing world. By focusing on these key areas, Enterprise Architecture can continue to be a strategic enabler that drives business growth, innovation, and resilience.

About The Author

Ian Loe

Ian has more than 28 years of experience in the IT industry with wide industry experience spannin public sector to financial services He has extensive experience in Enterprise Architecture combinec with deep knowledge in both infrastructure and application development.

Ian has served as CIO, CTO & CISO in large conglomerates and have deep experience in managing architecture, cybersecurity, infrastructure & data engineering teams for various organisations. Ian has introduced many modern approaches to technology management including implementing Hyper Converged Infrastructure (HCI), DevSecOps, FinOps, SRE, Risk Based Management, and the use of Breach & Attack Simulation (BAS) platforms.

He has held other senior appointments such as Director, Government Cybersecurity Operations and was responsible for managing cybersecurity operations for the whole of government in Singapore, which includes the monitoring of and response to cybersecurity incidents. He is also an regular industry speaker on many topics and an active adjunct senior fellow at the Singapore University of Technology & Design (SUTD).

Made in the USA
Monee, IL
24 September 2024

66455344R00233